I AM
I CAN
I WILL

'When I met Gerry I was totally stuck in the "I am" part of my life, hounded by demons from my past. He guided me through the "I Can" and eventually onto the "I Will" parts of my mindset. Without him, not only would I not have won the most competitive offshore sailing event in the world, but most of all I would not have enjoyed doing it and I would not be happy. His openness and authenticity, combined with his depth of knowledge of the human mind, make him an incredible person to work with.'

Tom Dolan, Irish solo sailor and winner of La Solitaire du Figaro Paprec, renowned as the toughest single-handed multistage offshore sailing race in the world

I AM

SILENCE YOUR INNER CRITIC

I CAN

WAKE UP YOUR INNER COACH

I WILL

RECLAIM YOUR CONFIDENCE AND POWER

GERRY HUSSEY

GILL BOOKS

Gill Books
Hume Avenue
Park West
Dublin 12
www.gillbooks.ie

Gill Books is an imprint of M.H. Gill and Co.

978 180458 2152
Designed by Sarah McCoy
Edited by Catherine Gough
Copyedited by Emma Dunne
Proofread by Esther Ní Dhonnacha
Printed and bound in Great Britain by Clays Ltd, Elcograf S.p.A.
This book is typeset in Utopia Regular.

*The paper used in this book comes from the wood pulp
of sustainably managed forests.*

The information given in this book should not be treated
as a substitute for professional medical advice; always
consult a medical practitioner.

To the best of our knowledge, this book complies in full with
the requirements of the General Product Safety Regulation
(GPSR). For further information and help with any safety
queries, please contact us at productsafety@gill.ie.

A CIP catalogue record for this book is available from the
British Library.

5 4 3 2 1

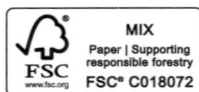

GERRY HUSSEY is a No. 1 bestselling author, speaker, performance coach and facilitator in the field of corporate leadership. With a background in psychology and performance coaching, he has been working with clients, sports professionals and teams for more than twenty years, inspiring and motivating them to reach their full potential. His previous books, *Awaken Your Power Within* and *The Freedom Within*, were bestsellers. Together with his wife Miriam Hussey, he is the founder of Soul Space, an empowering movement for awakening inner potential and inspiring greater health and performance through integrative mind, body and soul programs, speaking engagements and events.

ALSO BY THE AUTHOR
The Freedom Within
Awaken Your Power Within

CONTENTS

Our deepest fear is not that we are inadequate.
Our deepest fear is that we are powerful beyond measure.
It is our light, not our darkness that most frightens us.
We ask ourselves, 'Who am I to be brilliant, gorgeous,
talented, fabulous?'
Actually, who are you not to be?
You are a child of God.
Your playing small does not serve the world.
There's nothing enlightened about shrinking,
so that other people won't feel insecure around you.
We are all meant to shine, as children do.
We were born to make manifest the glory of God
that is within us.
It's not just in some of us; it's in everyone.
And as we let our own light shine,
we unconsciously give other people
permission to do the same.
As we're liberated from our own fear, our presence
automatically liberates others.

– MARIANNE WILLIAMSON

A NOTE FROM THE AUTHOR

In my first two books, *Awaken Your Power Within* and *The Freedom Within*, I took the approach of writing each book to encompass and explore a wide number of ideas. I wanted each of those books to set out my stall about my fascination with, and the breadth and depth of topics it takes to truly understand, the human being – its magnificence, its truth, its potential and, ultimately, the things that hold us back. I wanted to explore the science and show that very often it is mind-blowing, and that there are still so many aspects of the human being and the human mind that science can't understand.

In those books, we dealt with over 40 different topics, from the mind–body connection, the gut–brain axis, the nervous system and brain chemistry to conscious and unconscious programming. We explored the truth about emotions and dealt with the physical, biological and chemical impact every single emotion has on our health and well-being.

I wanted to give the reader an expansive view of the human being, of all the different aspects and all the different dimensions. I wanted to show that in order to be successful and happy and liberated, we need a multidimensional approach.

I also wanted to demonstrate that when dealing with things like anxiety or depression, or any form of illness, just as the cause can be multidimensional, it is equally important that we have a multidimensional plan when it comes to healing and recovery.

Having reflected on those two books and been overwhelmed by their success, I felt a calling to follow up with something that is connected to both of them. I also wanted to follow up with a book that is connected to my passion about how important it is to see ourselves and our lives from a multidimensional viewpoint, a book that speaks to the truth of our infinite possibilities – once we are prepared to release all that no longer serves us.

I wanted this book to be a continuation of the incredible journey that I am on myself, and the incredible journey that I am taking my readers on, and yet, while knowing this book should be a continuation and an expansion of my previous work, my heart was telling me that it should be different.

I then asked myself, if I were to write a book on just one thing, which topic do I truly believe would have the greatest impact not just on our happiness but also on our health and our ability to manifest the life we dream of?

When I meditated about this book, something kept appearing in my heart: the topic of our inner voice. And as I sat with it, as I explored why that would be the book I would write next, I realised that if we were to focus on *one* thing that could change our lives, *one* thing that could begin the liberation of our souls, it would be changing our self-talk.

A NOTE FROM THE AUTHOR

If we can change our inner self-talk, our inner voice, then something magnificent will happen.

I'm not saying that changing your inner voice is the cornerstone of everything and the only thing we need to do, but I am absolutely saying that changing the nature, tone, habits and patterns of our inner voice is one of the greatest gifts we can give ourselves. Because when we change the nature and tone of our inner voice, we are also changing the nature and tone of our health, the way in which we experience the world, the way in which others experience us and our ability to manifest the life we desire.

Writing this book has been an extraordinary gift, an opportunity for me to explore my inner voice, to really focus on the words I use every day when I communicate with myself, when I communicate with others, when I communicate with the universe. I have rediscovered the importance of developing an inner story that is not one of pain but one of power. A story that inspires, empowers and uplifts. A story that speaks to my dreams, not my fears.

Whether you are familiar with my work or are coming to it fresh, I hope this book connects and resonates with you, that it both challenges you and gives you a practical guide to transforming one of the most important and powerful things you possess: your inner voice.

I hope you enjoy it.
Gerry

INTRODUCTION: BELIEVE IT, LIVE IT, EXPERIENCE IT

Breathe, relax, soften. Eye on the ball, you've got this. Stay calm, stay strong. This is your time. Now go, protect the ball, accelerate, breathe, open. See the space, magnify the space, and now release the ball into the space. It's easy.

What is this, you might ask? What ball, what space, soften what? This is the inner voice of an athlete I worked with who scored one of the greatest goals in his sport.

While the words above give you an insight into the focus that he had within, outside of this calm, process-driven voice is a stadium of people screaming with all their hearts, creating a deafening wall of sound. Around him, players and coaches are shouting an array of instructions, and the massive scoreboard tells him that his team are losing and time is up. If he misses this shot, his team loses the championship. A lifetime of hopes for the fans and the dreams of his teammates sit firmly on his shoulders.

Everything outside of him is noise, chaos, adversity and pressure, telling him that there is no hope, only threat. Yet everything inside of him is silent, calm and focused, his senses telling him that there *is* time and there *is* hope and opportunity.

To many, this is a once-in-a-lifetime shot, a shot they have never taken before and might never get a chance to take again. But to him, this is a shot he has hit a thousand times, and he knows it only ends in one way: with him scoring.

In the months leading up to this split second, he had spent hundreds of hours visualising, mentally rehearsing and emotionally preparing for it. He had reprogrammed his inner story, which reprogrammed his entire belief system. He had done this by listening to an audio of specially chosen statements that ended with a very important one: 'I am an elite player, I am powerful and strong, I back myself in every situation, and I *will* have a massive impact on this season.'

But what made this even more spectacular is that for the months previous, he had not been a starting player on the team. In fact, he was facing being dropped out of the panel.

Rather than getting angry or giving up, he had decided this was the biggest opportunity of his life. Everything in his heart and soul demanded that he do whatever he could to get back on that team.

He broke his training down into every possible area: physical, technical, tactical and mental. And every day, he made sure he was getting better and better in each of those key areas. He had a deep belief that if he could get back on the team, he could have a massive impact and create something special, not just for the team but also for the people in his community, the people he cared deeply about.

We created a special audio for him, one that focused on him expressing himself, on becoming the greatest player he could be: 'I am an elite player, I am powerful and strong, I back myself in every single situation, and when my opportunity arises I will execute it.'

On the day of the game, he was not selected to start. In fact, it seemed highly unlikely that he would even feature. Yet that morning, with his usual strength, courage and passion, he turned up mentally, physically and technically. He was ready and prepared to play. He told himself he would have a massive impact on the season. When the ball came to him at that critical moment he was now fulfilling a prophecy, he was stepping into something he had visualised a thousand times, so there was no shred of doubt or distraction. He had seen it, lived it, experienced it, and now he simply had to execute it ...

*

It is so important in life that we never allow distraction or self-doubt to become our dominant story. Yes, life can be difficult. Yes, there will be setbacks. Yes, there will be tough times. But we should never lose sight of the most important story – that you are powerful, you are free, and you can have a massive impact not just on your own life but also on the lives of others.

It is through our inner stories that we can realise this. This player showed the world the power of inner stories. To be able to access this incredible voice at a moment that mattered was something he had worked on for a long time. He meditated every day to expand his focus and concentration skills, and he worked consistently at transforming his inner voice so that it was now solution-focused and opportunity-driven and directed him to his own greatness.

In my work with elite athletes, from world champions to Olympic champions, we cover many skills, but perhaps the greatest one we work on is reshaping and reprogramming our inner voice so that it is our asset, not our enemy. So that when we really need it, it turns up.

In my own life, the greatest gift I have given myself is an inner voice that empowers me, that magnifies solutions and opportunities, and is full of self-compassion and forgiveness. An inner voice that allows me to let go of the past quickly. I have worked hard to create an inner voice that speaks with clarity and calmness in times of great challenge.

At the start of all my events, I let participants know that the most important thing they will hear that day is not my voice or the meditations we use or the music we play. All of these are merely mechanisms through which they can access the most important voice of all: their inner voice, the voice of their truest being, the voice of the heart and soul.

We live in a world where people are constantly looking outward for advice and direction, constantly seeking external noise to distract and motivate them, which leads them to believe that all the important voices are outside. The outer world is so noisy that our inner voice gets lost and becomes an unconscious soundtrack to our lives, impacting so many aspects of our lives, and often we don't even know it. Therefore we can't let it go unchecked.

Do you have a dream that is still waiting to be manifested? Is there a challenge you want to overcome? Is there something from your past you want to let go of? Do you have a vision of yourself that you know you can be? The foundation to making all of these things possible is transforming your inner voice.

In the course of this book, I will help you explore and understand your inner voice, its habits and patterns, by asking questions such as:

* Is that voice enabling or disabling you?

* Is it empowering or disempowering you?

* Is it healing or hurting you?

* Is it the soundtrack you want to be listening to for the rest of your life?

* Is it time to transform and empower your inner voice?

As we discover and explore in greater detail, this inner voice provides us with the soundtrack to our lives. If our inner voice is a soundtrack that allows us to live a life of joy and adventure, let's turn up that music and make sure that we are living in alignment with the rhythm of our hearts. If we discover that this inner voice is a soundtrack that is actually holding us back and keeping us trapped in unhelpful emotions, then I will show you how to not just scratch the record but actually change the record and start listening to a whole new tune.

If you are ready to examine your inner voice, its patterns and habits, then this is the book for you. If you want to discover where this inner voice came from and when it began, whether you selected it yourself or it was given to you, then this is the book for you. And, finally, if it's time to change the record, then this is the book for you.

I'm going to help you reframe your inner voice so that it is driving you forward instead of holding you back. The steps to achieving this are in your hands, and they are simple. I only ask that you make a promise to yourself that you will be consistent and that you will commit to giving yourself this incredible gift because you matter, your dreams matter, and your health matters. Let's make a commitment to awaken a new inner voice – one of love, passion, forgiveness, compassion and empowerment. An inner voice that says:

I am.

I can.

I will.

During our exploration I will use the term 'inner voice' to refer to the voice we hear when we listen to the way we speak to ourselves. Our inner voice refers to the tone and nature of the voice we hear within. I will use the term 'inner narrative' to refer to the story that that voice is telling us. Through real life stories, and the incredible lessons to be learned from them, we will examine our inner voice from three perspectives:

1. What it is, why we have one and how it is formed.

2. The things that can perpetuate an old, outdated and even hurtful inner voice and inner narrative, and prevent us from challenging and changing it.

3. The incredibly simple and powerful tools we can use each and every day to change our inner voice and our inner narrative so that we can finally let go of an inner voice that no longer serves us.

I will also introduce you to incredible, simple techniques, such as the A-method, that allow us to take control of both our inner voice and inner narrative in a stressful situation or moment and, through a few powerful steps, ensure we are communicating in a way that moves us from disempowerment to empowerment, from victimhood to victory.

To get the most out of this book, I would suggest reading it through once in full and then reading it again, working through the exercises, meditations and visualisations one by one, coming back to the ones that have the biggest impact on you again and again.

Now is the time to honour this commitment. Throughout this book, I will ask you to put pen to paper to observe and record that inner voice and gradually begin to change it. By doing so I promise that you will gain new understanding, new habits and a new ability to move forward in life with more ease. The first step in making a change is signing your name. It's a contract with yourself to put the techniques and approaches in this book into practice and a statement of your intention to reframe your inner voice.

_____

Sign your name here

SECTION 1:

I AM

SECTION 2:

I CAN

SECTION 3:

I WILL

CHAPTER 1
KNOW THYSELF

Apathy or action? Victim or victory?

'There's no point applying for that job, I wouldn't get it anyway'; 'I'll never meet anyone – everyone is already coupled up'; 'I'll never recover from my injury in time to compete in the race'. Does any of this sound familiar to you? Have you ever chosen apathy instead of action? Many of us miss out on opportunities because our inner voice is feeding us a false narrative to keep us within the limits of the past and the limits of our fears. The first step to changing that narrative is discovering what it is, knowing where that voice comes from and what has influenced and shaped it.

First, we're going to look at that voice that tells us who we are – the 'I AM'. When we make the 'I am' statement, we can sometimes think of what follows the 'I am' as some form of fixed or static entity that can't be changed. For example, some people say 'I'm not musical', 'I'm not good at maths', 'I'm not confident', 'I'm not good with money,' as if it's an in-built part of their personality. Yet the science has proven that so many of our skill sets and so much of our personality can actually be changed. Therefore, we need to be very careful when we make 'I am' statements. The truth is, no matter what you might be today, you are not stuck with being that for the rest of your life. The most important 'I am' statements are:

I am capable of incredible change.

I am ready and willing to let go of all old and conditioned beliefs about myself.

I am ready to start again.

I am capable of extraordinary growth and transformation.

Before we can become something, we need to see it and believe it and be able to speak future truth about the person we are committed to becoming.

The beginning of your journey to positive change can be summed up by the famous Greek maxim: 'Know thyself'. So, let's get cracking.

What is your inner voice?

Every single one of us has an inner voice. It is a powerful tool that shapes our perceptions, decisions and beliefs. Whether we are aware of it or not, our inner voice is not just commenting on the world around us: it is also directing our awareness, our attention, and impacting our decisions. By understanding its origins, recognising its influence and actively working on improving and enhancing it, we can cultivate a more positive and empowering inner self-talk that can help us navigate life's challenges with greater resilience and well-being.

The two internal voices: chatterbox and deeper wisdom

The inner voice, as a whole, is made up of two internal voices: the chatterbox of the brain and the deepest wisdom of the soul. The chatterbox feeds the ego; our deeper wisdom feeds our soul.

The voice of the thinking brain mainly operates as a threat-detection system. It is always looking for real threats, potential threats and even previous threats. This voice of the thinking brain is an active and consistent commentary designed to keep you away from not just real threats, but even perceived and imagined threats.

I call this voice the 'chatterbox': it is a constant stream of thoughts, some intelligent, some based in fact, though often many of its words and stories are neither intelligent nor based in fact.

The chatterbox is like a young child just learning language: the child desperately wants to speak and be heard so they use whatever words and sentences they have at their disposal, which often results in a stream of incoherent speech that has not been thought out. It is simply based on the child's need to be seen and loved, as well as their impulsive need for instant gratification and to have their opinion listened to.

The chatterbox is a conditioned program. It has been conditioned by our life experiences, by people of significance in our lives, by events we have witnessed, moments we have experienced and societal norms. The chatterbox is a totally constructed and temporary program, and its key purpose is survival and safety and to feed the needs of the ego. We will do a brief but insightful dive into the human ego a little later – what it is, why we have it, the benefits of

17

it and the potential downfalls of listening to and feeding it (see p. 57).

The second voice is an inner knowing and powerful intuition that is far deeper than the chatterbox of the thinking brain. **This deeper voice is at all times connected to a truth: it always knows right from wrong, knows the way we should proceed in any situation and will always lead you home.** This deeper inner wisdom is not interested in feeding the ego and is only interested in feeding our soul. It is the voice of our true self: it is the voice of love, compassion, non-attachment and non-comparison.

Therefore, the greatest challenge we will ever face as human beings is not seeking to know the right thing to do; the greatest challenge is convincing the voice in your head that what is in your heart is the right thing to do. We need to allow ourselves the freedom to follow our hearts without having to worry about, give in to or be distracted by the noise of our chatterbox.

We will always have a chatterbox – a running commentary of the brain that is driven by fear and committed to defence. It's the voice that wants to criticise, wants to compare, wants to judge, wants to play it safe, wants to hold us back. But with a little work and understanding, we can get to a point where this chatterbox voice quietens. And with a little more work, we can get to a point where we don't really care if it's loud or not because we know it's just our chatterbox, it's just our ego, it's just our deepest fear operating in another form. While we are fully aware of this voice, we know that we are neither that voice nor are we defined by or victims of it. We don't have to engage with it or act on it because we also have a voice of deeper wisdom and truth, which always knows the right thing to do. We can reach a point where we are wise enough to know which voice is to be ignored and which voice is to be engaged with.

The 'lizard brain' refers to a concept in neuroscience related to the most primitive part of our brain, often associated with the limbic system or reptilian brain. This part of the brain regulates the most basic survival instincts and primal impulses in humans.

The concept of the lizard brain stems from the idea that our brains have evolved in layers over millions of years. The limbic system, or lizard brain, is among the oldest parts, dating back to when our ancestors were reptiles. It is primarily responsible for regulating survival instincts, including fight-or-flight responses, emotions, and basic drives such as hunger, thirst and sexual desire. These instincts are essential for survival and are largely unconscious and automatic.

The limbic system plays a crucial role in processing emotions and forming emotional memories. It influences emotional responses to stimuli and helps in decision-making based on past experiences and instincts.

The lizard brain operates through neurotransmitters such as dopamine, serotonin and adrenaline, which regulate mood, emotions and arousal levels. These chemical messengers shape behaviour and responses to the environment. The lizard brain can override more rational or logical decision-making processes in certain situations, especially when faced with threats or stressful stimuli. This can lead to impulsive or instinctual reactions that prioritise survival over reasoning.

The thinking self and inner knowing

The thinking self and inner knowing are two different aspects of our consciousness that play a role in how we perceive and navigate the world.

The thinking self is the part of our consciousness that is responsible for analysing, reasoning, problem-solving and making decisions based on logic and past experiences. It is the voice in our head that constantly provides commentary, judgements and interpretations of our thoughts, emotions and experiences. The thinking self is heavily influenced by our beliefs, conditioning and societal norms, and it often operates from a place of fear, self-doubt and limiting beliefs. But if our thoughts or emotions become overly negative then we distort the thinking self's sense of perspective and balance and we instead turn it into a threat detection system.

The constant interruption of our inner stories disrupts our ability to simply experience life and other people as they are without judgement. This is what prevents so many of us from being 'in the moment'. The thinking self prevents us from observing things with an open mind and with love, and instead fills the moment with fear, distraction and noise. This inner commentary can greatly decrease our quality of life and fill our precious moments with narratives and fears that often have very little grounding in reality. It's as though we are at the most beautiful orchestral recital in the world, but instead of being able to hear it, it is drowned out by our inner soundtrack of fear. The universe, the present moment, is the orchestra, and we're often unable to experience it as it is because of the deafening commentary going on in our heads.

On the other hand, inner knowing, also referred to as intu-ition, gut feeling or inner wisdom, is the more intuitive part of ourselves that transcends logic and rationality. It is a source of inner guidance, wisdom and clarity that arises from a deeper understanding of ourselves and our connection to the universe. Inner knowing tends to be more subtle, gentle and peaceful compared to the often loud and critical voice of the thinking self. It can provide insights, solutions and a sense of direction that go beyond what the rational mind can comprehend.

In essence, when the thinking self is working well, it operates from a place of analysis, judgement and logic, while inner knowing operates from a place of intuition, wisdom and connection to a deeper truth. Both aspects of our consciousness play important roles in our lives, and learning to balance and integrate them can lead to a more harmonious and fulfilling existence.

Self-talk and our nervous system

As well as creating our external reality and our experience of the world, our inner voice has a direct and real impact on our physical health through the role it plays in the activation of our nervous system. The nervous system is like the body's internal communication network, constantly sending messages between the brain, spinal cord and the rest of the body. It helps us respond to the world around us, while also playing a key role in stress management.

This complex network of nerves, cells and tissues is divided into two main parts: the central nervous system (CNS) and the peripheral nervous system (PNS).

Central nervous system (CNS)

The CNS consists of the brain and spinal cord. It serves as the control centre for the entire body, processing information from the senses, making decisions and sending out commands. The brain plays a crucial role in cognitive functions, emotions, memory and voluntary movements, while the spinal cord serves as a pathway for information flow between the brain and the peripheral nerves.

Peripheral nervous system (PNS)

The PNS includes all the nerves extending from the CNS to the rest of the body. It is further divided into the somatic nervous system, which controls voluntary movements and sensory functions; and the autonomic nervous system, which regulates involuntary processes such as heart rate, digestion and respiration.

Our inner voice and self-talk are thought to originate from various and specific regions of the brain, such as the prefrontal cortex, the temporal lobes and the auditory cortex. These areas are involved in language processing, self-referential thinking and memory, which all contribute to our inner dialogues. This inner voice and inner narrative can have a significant impact on our nervous system, which is responsible for regulating our body's responses to stress and managing our emotions, thoughts and behaviours. Because the brain cannot tell the difference between what we are thinking about and what is actually happening, when we engage in negative self-talk and use words that are threat- and fear-based, the brain believes they must be real and imminent threats, so it prepares itself for defence and activates the body's stress response, which impacts our nervous system in various ways:

* Fight or flight response: Negative self-talk can trigger the body's fight or flight response, activating the sympathetic

nervous system. This can lead to the release of stress hormones such as cortisol and adrenaline, preparing the body to respond to perceived threats. Chronic activation of this response can contribute to anxiety, high blood pressure and other stress-related health issues.

* Immune system: Negative self-talk can suppress the immune system, making us more susceptible to illness and reducing our ability to fight off infections. Chronic stress and negative self-talk can weaken the immune system over time, leading to a higher risk of developing chronic health conditions.

* Emotional regulation: Our self-talk can also influence our ability to regulate our emotions. Negative self-talk can exacerbate feelings of anxiety, depression and over-whelm, making it harder to manage our emotions effectively. This can lead to mood swings, irritability and difficulty coping with stress.

* Pain perception: Negative self-talk can affect our perception of pain. Research has shown that people who engage in negative self-talk may experience increased sensitivity to pain, whereas those who practise positive self-talk may have a higher pain tolerance.

* Overall well-being: Our self-talk can have a profound impact on our well-being and quality of life. Negative self-talk can contribute to feelings of low self-esteem, self-doubt and negative self-image, while positive self-talk can boost confidence, self-worth and resilience.

By cultivating positive self-talk and self-compassion, we can help regulate our nervous system and promote greater emotional well-being and emotional resilience.

Our inner voice primes our reticular activating system and we create our own self-fulfilling echo chamber

The reticular activating system (RAS) is located in the brainstem and plays a crucial role in regulating arousal, attention and consciousness. It acts as a filter for incoming sensory information, determining what stimuli to pay attention to and what to ignore. Positive self-talk can help us focus on our goals and priorities, enhancing our ability to concentrate on what we want and not what we fear, and stay motivated towards that goal. Conversely, negative self-talk can distract us and drain our mental energy, making it harder to focus on tasks. The RAS plays a role in setting and achieving goals by prioritising information that aligns with our objectives. Positive self-talk can help us set realistic and achievable goals, enhancing our motivation and persistence. Negative self-talk, on the other hand, can create self-doubt and undermine our confidence, making it harder to stay motivated and take action towards our goals.

The RAS is connected to areas of the brain which regulate emotions, such as the amygdala and prefrontal cortex. Our RAS also plays a vital role in our self-perception and self-image. It filters information about ourselves based on our beliefs and self-talk. Positive self-talk can reinforce a positive self-image and boost self-esteem, influencing how we perceive ourselves and our abilities. Negative self-talk can distort our self-perception and reinforce limiting beliefs, leading to feelings of inadequacy or self-criticism.

Our self-talk reflects our underlying beliefs about ourselves, our capabilities and the world around us. If we consistently tell ourselves negative and limiting narratives, we are likely to attract circumstances that confirm those beliefs. Conversely, positive and empowering self-talk can help us align our beliefs with our desires and attract opportunities that support our goals.

By cultivating positive self-talk and practising mindfulness, we can help regulate the activity of the RAS and promote greater focus, emotional well-being and motivation. Engaging in positive affirmations, visualisation techniques and cognitive-behavioural strategies can help reprogram our brain for positivity and support our overall mental health and performance.

For instance, take the following scenario of a golfer on a tee box playing into a narrow fairway beside a big bunker.

Threat-based thinking	RAS activity	Outcome
'Don't hit the bunker. If I hit the bunker, I'm in trouble.'	Fear–stress centre of the brain is activated.	Our swing is poor because the body is tense.
'I'm terrible at taking these shots.'	Prefrontal cortex closes down.	We rush the shot.
	Visual field is reduced to focus only on the threat.	We are so focused on the bunker that that's where we hit the ball.
	The body tightens, restricting the swing.	We activate our stress response even further.
	Breathing becomes fast and shallow, taking us out of a flow state.	

Opportunity-based thinking	RAS activity	Outcome
'If I hit that area of the fairway, I'm in a great position.'	Calm response.	A beautiful swing.
	Enthusiastic and hopeful feeling.	A perfectly timed shot.
'This is a perfect opportunity.'	Prefrontal cortex stays open and we maintain creativity and perspective.	We are so focused on the fairway that we deliver the ball onto the fairway.
'I'm excellent at taking these opportunities.'	The body remains loose.	Drives enthusiasm and self-confidence.
	Breath is slow and deep.	
	We stay in a flow state.	

Theta brainwaves and our inner narrative

As many of us know, the human brain has a series of brainwave activities that we move in and out of on a continuous basis. We have certain brainwave activities that are responsible for certain feelings and thoughts, and while we are absolutely meant to move between them, we are not meant to be stuck in them. As we will discover, some are more helpful than others.

There are four main brainwave frequencies that the human brain moves through:

1. **Gamma brainwave:** This relates to concentration and composure.

2. **Beta brainwave:** This relates to more stressful states of thinking and feelings. Beta brainwave is associated with

anxiety-dominant thinking, active and external attention focus, worst-case scenario planning, thought fixation and a sense that something bad is about to happen.

3. **Alpha brainwave:** When we are in alpha brainwave, we are more relaxed, and we have a passive attention state. We are more curious and we are able to observe a situation without the need to respond to it.

4. **Theta brainwave:** A deeply relaxed, inward-focused state of thinking and feeling. Theta brainwave is almost like a meditation state of flow. When we are in theta brainwave, we can download and process information quickly.

Between birth and eight years old, we predominantly operate from theta brainwave. This is why a young child can download so much information about themselves and the world quickly, and it is why most young children have an active sense of fun and play with ease.

The only challenge with theta brainwave is that we are downloading information so quickly that we don't really assess or analyse it deeply. In the absence of this level of assessment, we can believe everything we download, which is why young children are more likely to believe in fictional characters and fictional stories.

At this early stage of our lives, our subconscious programs and beliefs are also being downloaded. For most of us, 90 per cent of our subconscious beliefs are downloaded and in place by the time we are eight years old, and many of us can spend the rest of our adult lives living within the limits of these programs and beliefs.

This is why the age of eight is so important. When we seek to understand our true identity, our deepest beliefs and the unconscious blockers that we have as adults, we realise these can be traced back to moments, situations and scenarios we were immersed in or exposed to before we were eight years old.

An extension of these subconscious programs is our inner voice. Whether we know it or not, much of the habits and patterns of the inner voice we live with as adults were, in fact, learned when we were in this theta brainwave state between the ages of zero and eight.

Functions of our inner voice: why we talk to ourselves

Now that we are beginning to see the importance of our inner voice and how empowering or disempowering it can be, we realise that our inner voice needs to be consistently worked on and trained. Initially, this might feel like another piece of work we have to do, another task we have to take on when we are already so busy. We might think:

Would it be better if we didn't have an inner voice?

What if there was no chatter going on inside my head?

What if I wasn't analysing the world and people around me?

Wouldn't it be better to not have an inner voice at all?

Well, the truth is, when we examine why we have our inner voice, we become aware of how important it is and that it serves so many functions for us. Our inner voice plays a role in many aspects that are vital to our existence, our survival, our understanding and our ability to live an incredible life.

So, let's take a look at some of the key functions of our inner voice.

Memory: we repeat things in our mind

Many of us may have experienced babies as they begin to develop language and start to repeat words, especially new words, over and over. They often repeat these new words both out loud and internally. This is part of their learning process. We might have experienced it ourselves as adults, perhaps while studying for exams or even by repeating shopping lists so we don't forget.

Fact-checking: we repeat things to see if they feel true

When we hear new information, the brain likes to repeat it again and again to see if it can make sense of it, understand it and believe it. You might have noticed that if you were in an argument and someone said something that annoyed you or that you didn't agree with, you have a natural reaction to repeat that statement. Our brain will run and re-run stories until we either accept them or decide that they are not true.

Adaptability: the ability to understand and deal with the curveballs life can throw at us

In a fast-paced, ever-changing world, psychological adaptability is a critical skill for being able to live with ease and confidence.

Psychological adaptation is a functional, cognitive or behavioural trait that helps an organism to survive and thrive in its environment. It falls under the scope of evolved psychological mechanisms, which relate to our capacity to make appropriate responses to changed or changing situations.

In essence, it is the ability to modify or adjust our thinking, feelings and behaviour in meeting different circumstances or different people, or our ability to meet a similar situation with new thinking when we encounter it for a second or third time.

People who are adaptable tend to be flexible, resilient and open to change. Psychological adaptability means we don't get stuck in a fixed mindset or belief system, and we can easily adapt our thinking and feelings when we are dealing with change and uncertainty.

The bidirectional loop of our subconscious mind

There is a powerful connection between our inner stories and our subconscious beliefs, and it is a strong bidirectional loop. Our subconscious programs and inner talk are interconnected in the sense that our subconscious beliefs, thoughts and emotions influence the content and tone of our inner dialogue. The subconscious mind stores our past experiences, beliefs and habits, which can impact the way we perceive ourselves and the world around us. These subconscious programs can manifest in the form of self-limiting beliefs, negative self-talk or self-sabotaging behaviours. Only when we explore our deepest subconscious beliefs and programs does our inner voice make sense, and when we begin to change our deepest subconscious beliefs, we begin to also change our inner voice to match them.

By becoming aware of and addressing these subconscious patterns, we can work towards cultivating a more positive and empowering inner dialogue.

A quick overview of our subconscious mind

The primary function of the subconscious mind is to allow us to make fast decisions as we go about our daily lives. To do this it uses fast reflex decisions; it doesn't value stopping to assess and reflect on what is actually going on and what a new and better response might be. It is not interested in the best possible reaction – it's simply interested in not dying and in sticking with the familiar.

Our subconscious programs are what keep us in a self-perpetuating sense of a familiar and constructed vision of the world, of ourselves and of what's going to happen. To the subconscious mind, the familiar breeds trust, comfort and loyalty. It simply wants to help you make a fast, familiar decision that enables it to fulfil its expectations and beliefs about you and the world.

In many ways, your subconscious programs are like a plane on autopilot flying to a pre-decided location. The location is our subconscious beliefs; the autopilot is our subconscious mind; the subconscious programs ensure we take the necessary actions and decisions to arrive at that pre-decided location.

The subconscious programs are the hardwired, and often outdated, thinking and behavioural habits. They are based on past experiences and are committed to ensuring our life arrives at the same point, regardless of the outside environment or the infinite number of places it could go.

With every experience you have in life – especially the highly emotive ones that involve fear, shame or guilt – you create intense conclusions about these events and situations, and you store the messages that will drive your future actions should a similar situation arise again.

We subconsciously manipulate our perception of events and opportunities to avoid the people, places and opportunities where pain was located in the past or where we perceive it may be located in the future.

If at some stage in your childhood you felt or perceived that you were rejected by someone, this could have created an internal high emotional response that you stored in your memory. If you experience a similar situation at a later stage in your life, your subconscious mind will quickly search your memories for all the times you felt rejected and will start to replay the same thought process and response you had as a child. This will reactivate the fears or beliefs that you are somehow unworthy or undeserving.

The amazing thing is that even if we experience a situation that goes against our internal subconscious beliefs, we will manipulate and sabotage the situation to ensure the end outcome fits those subconscious beliefs. For example, if you meet someone who finds you attractive and there is the possibility of a great relationship with this person, but you believe they couldn't find you attractive or that they wouldn't love the *real* you, when the relationship fails to happen, or does happen but eventually fails, we will tell ourselves, 'I knew that wasn't going to work.' Our love life has just fallen victim to our deepest inner beliefs.

The next time someone says something you perceive as an insult or a slight, take a moment to examine the situation. Was the comment directed at you personally? What emotional state was the person saying it in? Was their intention to hurt you or offend you – and where is your assumption that they intended to hurt you coming from? Are you taking the comment the wrong way because they are triggering an emotion or a subconscious belief in you?

Self-sabotage is not a negative act; it's a protective act of your subconscious mind to stop you from experiencing potential failure or hurt.

This doesn't just apply to highly emotive situations. Your subconscious mind is constantly downloading the decisions and habits you make even in everyday normal activities. It stores these as 'the way we do things' so that they become automatic: the route we take to work, the coffee we order, the television shows we watch, the side of the bed we sleep on ... We build up a set of habits and often don't know why, but we rarely go against them. Even thinking about changing them can bring up a feeling of unease.

In many ways, the subconscious is the very thing that prevents us from doing things differently, and it's happy if we keep getting the same result, even if it is not the result we want. In committing to new ways of thinking, behaving and creating a new life vision, we will have to overcome our subconscious mind. It will tell us all types of stories to get us to fall back into our familiar past: 'You had a good week of nutrition, and you went to the gym so, go on, you deserve a night of chocolate and wine'; 'You went on a holiday with a loved one and you had loads of romantic walks that you enjoyed, but then you came home and stopped doing them'; 'You signed up for a charity 5k and loved training for it, but then, when the event was over, you stopped running and went back to your old ways.'

We need to break away from a state of conditioned habits and reflexes, and achieve a state of conscious decision-making where we are free to make new choices and achieve a new reality. We need to break the cycle of the conditioned programs and stories that are running in our minds. We need to change the record in order to hear a new song.

Self-esteem

Self-esteem is a fundamental quality for living a healthy and joyful life. Yet many people struggle with the lack of it. The ability to appreciate and honour oneself, to recognise one's own worth, value and capabilities, forms the cornerstone of mental and emotional well-being and builds a strong and healthy foundation from which we can interact with others. Despite this, a high level and robust sense of self-esteem seems to be elusive for many, who often find themselves trapped by subconscious barriers that inhibit their ability to experience joy, fulfilment and the inherent wonder and magnificence that lies within them. The beginning point is to examine our current subconscious barriers and inhibitors so that we can first identify our deeply held subconscious beliefs that are often the real and true root cause of our limitations. The subconscious mind, unlike the conscious mind, does not judge, analyse or critique; it instead accepts any thought we send to it as absolute truth. **Changing what we feed our subconscious mind can lead to profound changes in our lives.**

To examine your current subconscious beliefs, I would like you to complete the following exercise. I will make a statement, and I would love for you to answer it. I want you to answer it by ticking the answer that immediately feels right. Use your instinct to answer.

1.   I am deeply loved.   YES

                                              MAYBE

                                              NO

2. I am deserving of great love.

    YES

    MAYBE

    NO

3. I take time to mind myself regularly.

    YES

    MAYBE

    NO

4. I am very comfortable in my own skin and in my own self.

    YES

    MAYBE

    NO

5. I am proud of who I see in the mirror.

    YES

    MAYBE

    NO

6. I am able to deal with challenging feedback in a healthy and open-minded way.

    YES

    MAYBE

    NO

7. I find it easy to write down 10 incredible things about myself.

    YES

    MAYBE

    NO

8. I speak kindly to myself when I make mistakes.

    YES

    MAYBE

    NO

9. I am proud of all my accomplishments and regularly take time to acknowledge them.

    YES

    MAYBE

    NO

10. I trust my inner instinct.

YES

MAYBE

NO

11. I am confident in my own abilities.

YES

MAYBE

NO

12. Great success awaits me.

YES

MAYBE

NO

13. I have the ability to attract great abundance into my life.

YES

MAYBE

NO

14. I allow myself to play regularly.

YES

MAYBE

NO

15. I don't take life too seriously.

YES

MAYBE

NO

16. I radiate beauty and kindness.

YES

MAYBE

NO

17. I trust the universe.

YES

MAYBE

NO

18. I trust myself.

YES

MAYBE

NO

19. I am all that I can be.

YES

MAYBE

NO

20. I am at peace within.

YES

MAYBE

NO

Now take a moment to examine your answers and see which ones you are secure and happy with and which ones you would like to be able to change. Do your answers surprise you? What does it feel like to say it out loud and see it written down?

Does seeing your answers to these types of statements help you to observe the patterns and habits in your self-talk, especially in times of stress and moments of great importance? The more we continue to examine our deepest beliefs, the more our self-talk habits and patterns make sense. They are never without reason and never without cause. The reasons and causes behind our self-talk can be many and varied, as we will discover, but understanding our deepest beliefs about ourselves is a great starting point. The aim is to take it in without judgement, and if there are any answers you would like to be different, we will work on how you can change that in the next sections.

Pattern matching

All too often, our external world is simply an extension of our inner beliefs. We can become hypersensitive to the external things that match our inner picture and totally blind to everything else. In psychology, this is called 'pattern matching'. It's a process by which the subconscious creates an inner picture based on a memory of a similar situation or your preconceived idea of how you expect a situation to go. When your subconscious mind has created this inner picture, your conscious mind will scan your environment and select only the things that match your inner, already-created picture, and it will ignore everything that doesn't. This often means you miss details and information that are right in front of you, and instead you select only the pieces that match your inner beliefs and expectations. In fact, much of your reality is a subjectively created version or an interpretation of reality that serves and meets your inner beliefs and stories.

Our subconscious programs are the thinking habits and mechanisms that the mind uses to fulfil our inner subconscious beliefs and expectations. **The scary thing is you spend up to 95 per cent of your day operating from subconscious programs and beliefs.** In committing to new ways of thinking and behaving, you will often have to overcome your single biggest enemy in the face of change: your subconscious mind. It will tell you all types of stories to get you to fall back into your familiar past.

The good news is that our subconscious beliefs can be adjusted and changed, and when we do this, we have a totally different experience of life.

Our self-talk plays a significant role in what we manifest in our life because our thoughts and beliefs shape our reality.

The concept of manifestation is closely tied to the law of attraction, which suggests that like attracts like – meaning that positive thoughts attract positive outcomes, while negative thoughts can bring about negative experiences. If we have an internal voice and an internal narrative that is consistent enough and loud enough, it can become an echo chamber that drowns out all other possibilities. Our self-talk can become a self-fulfilling prophecy, where our beliefs and thoughts shape our actions and behaviours, ultimately leading to the outcomes we manifest. So, let's make that self-fulfilling prophecy an empowering one.

CHAPTER 2
THE LIFE EXPERIENCES
THAT SHAPE US

Understanding where our inner voice comes from

Our inner voice is not shaped by one thing or one moment alone: our inner voice is a complex interplay of various factors, including our past experiences, our upbringing, cultural and societal influences and personal beliefs. It is in part formed through the messages we receive from our parents, teachers, peers and society at large, as well as our own interpretations of and reflections on those messages. These early experiences lay the foundation for our inner voice, creating a set of beliefs and attitudes that guide our thoughts and behaviours.

Let's take a deeper look at some of the most significant things that greatly shape and influence the nature, tone and patterns of our inner voice.

The inner voice of trauma

This is the voice of the wounded soul. Trauma can come in many shapes and versions; it can be one big event or experience or it can be lots of little setbacks, comments and experiences. Trauma refers to wounding – it can be physical wounding, but the most significant wounding is that of our soul, which is why emotional trauma is often the most difficult to heal. The incredible psychologist Gabor Maté says, 'Trauma is not what happened to you, trauma is what happens inside you when that thing happened.' **I believe one of the greatest traumas a human being can experience is the feeling of being unloved, unlovable and emotionally abandoned.**

The inner voice of someone with a wounded soul can be characterised by feelings of pain, sadness, unworthiness and self-blame. It may be filled with negative self-talk, self-criticism and self-doubt. This inner voice might constantly remind the person of past traumas, failures or hurts, leading to a sense of heaviness, hopelessness and despair.

The inner voice of someone with a wounded soul may also manifest as feelings of insecurity, fear and disconnection from others. They may struggle to trust themselves and others, and may have difficulty opening up or seeking help. This inner voice can magnify feelings of isolation and loneliness, making it challenging for the person to find healing and peace.

Trauma can have a profound impact on our inner voice and self-talk. The experience of trauma, whether physical, emotional or psychological, can shatter our sense of safety, trust and stability in self, in others or in the world, leading to lasting effects on our beliefs, behaviours and relationships. Trauma can disrupt the way we perceive ourselves, others and the world, shaping our inner voice in ways that are often negative, critical and self-destructive.

Individuals who have experienced trauma may develop beliefs about themselves as being fundamentally flawed, unworthy or powerless, leading to a pervasive inner voice that criticises and undermines their self-esteem and self-worth. This negative self-talk can reinforce feelings of shame, guilt and self-blame, perpetuating a cycle of emotional distress and self-destructive behaviours.

Trauma can also impact our ability to trust others and form healthy attachments, as the experience of betrayal or abandonment can lead to heightened fears of vulnerability and rejection. This can result in an inner voice that is constantly hypervigilant, warning us of potential dangers and threats in our relationships and environment.

Furthermore, trauma can dysregulate our emotional responses and coping mechanisms, leading to difficulties in managing stress, anxiety and depression. This can manifest as intrusive thoughts, flashbacks and nightmares, further fuelling negative self-talk and reinforcing beliefs of helplessness and hopelessness.

To address the impact of trauma on our inner voice, it is essential to seek therapy or counselling to process and heal from the traumatic experiences. Through trauma-informed therapy, individuals can explore and work through their emotions, thoughts and beliefs in a safe and supportive environment, learning to reframe negative self-talk patterns and cultivate greater self-compassion and resilience. Building a strong support network, engaging in self-care practices and developing healthy coping strategies can also help individuals navigate the impact of trauma on their inner voice and promote healing and growth.

Attachment plays a vital role in our self talk. There are three types of attachment: secure, insecure and avoidant. Below we will examine all three and how each impacts our self talk.

The inner voice of insecure attachment

Insecure attachment can have a significant impact on our inner voice and self-talk. Attachment theory, developed by psychologist John Bowlby, suggests that the quality of our early relationships with caregivers shapes our psychological development and influences our emotional and social functioning throughout our lives. When a child experiences inconsistent, neglectful or abusive caregiving, they may develop insecure attachment patterns that can carry over into adulthood and affect their inner voice in various ways.

Individuals with insecure attachment may struggle with feelings of worthlessness, inadequacy and fear of abandonment. These negative beliefs about themselves can manifest as critical and self-critical inner voices, constantly reminding them of their perceived flaws and shortcomings. This negative self-talk can fuel feelings of low self-esteem, self-doubt and self-blame, impacting their relationships, decision-making and overall well-being.

Insecure attachment can also lead to difficulties in forming healthy relationships and trusting others, as individuals may struggle to develop secure attachments with others due to their early experiences of inconsistent or unreliable caregiving. This can further exacerbate feelings of isolation, loneliness and self-criticism, reinforcing negative patterns of self-talk and beliefs about themselves and others.

Additionally, insecure attachment can result in difficulties regulating emotions and coping with stress, leading to heightened levels of anxiety, depression and other mental health challenges. These emotional struggles can further reinforce negative self-talk and undermine an individual's sense of self-worth and resilience.

To address the impact of insecure attachment on our inner voice, it is essential to engage in therapy or counselling to explore and work through these early attachment wounds. By developing greater self-awareness, challenging negative self-talk patterns and building healthier relationships based on trust and security, individuals can begin to cultivate a more positive and compassionate inner voice that supports their emotional well-being and overall growth.

The inner voice of avoidant attachment

Avoidant attachment is characterised by a reluctance to rely on others, a tendency to downplay emotions and a preference for independence and self-reliance. Individuals with avoidant attachment may have developed this pattern in response to inconsistent care or support from caregivers in early childhood, leading them to suppress their emotional needs and maintain emotional distance from others.

The impact of avoidant attachment on our inner voice can manifest in several ways.

* **Self-sufficiency:** Individuals with avoidant attachment may have an inner voice that emphasises self-reliance, independence and autonomy. They may downplay or dismiss their emotional needs, viewing vulnerability and

dependence as signs of weakness. Their internal dialogue may prioritise self-sufficiency and detachment, reinforcing a belief that they can only rely on themselves.

* **Emotional distancing:** Avoidant attachment can influence our inner voice by promoting emotional distancing and detachment from others. Individuals may have a critical or dismissive internal dialogue that devalues emotional expressiveness, intimacy and connection. Their inner voice may discourage vulnerability, emotional openness and seeking support from others, reinforcing a sense of emotional self-sufficiency.

* **Emotional suppression:** Individuals with avoidant attachment may struggle to acknowledge, identify and express their emotions, leading to emotional suppression and avoidance. Their inner voice may dismiss or minimise emotional experiences, labelling them as insignificant or irrelevant. This internal narrative can inhibit emotional expression, self-awareness and emotional regulation, contributing to difficulties in forming close relationships and understanding their own emotional needs.

* **Fear of intimacy:** Avoidant attachment can heighten a fear of intimacy and vulnerability in relationships, shaping our inner voice to prioritise self-protection and emotional distance. Individuals may have an internal dialogue that fears being dependent, vulnerable or rejected by others, reinforcing a belief that emotional closeness is risky or threatening. This internal narrative

can hinder the development of deep, meaningful connections and emotional intimacy with others.

* **Negative self-perceptions:** Avoidant attachment can influence our inner voice by fostering negative self-perceptions, self-criticism and self-doubt. Individuals may internalise beliefs of unworthiness, inadequacy or undesirability, shaping their inner dialogue to be harsh, self-critical or dismissive of their own needs and emotions. This internal narrative can undermine self-esteem, self-compassion and self-acceptance, contributing to a pervasive sense of emotional distance and disconnection from oneself and others.

Overall, avoidant attachment can impact our inner voice by promoting self-sufficiency, emotional distancing, suppression of emotions, fear of intimacy and negative self-perceptions. By recognising and addressing these patterns in our internal dialogue, individuals with avoidant attachment can work towards enhancing their emotional awareness, forming healthier relationships and cultivating a more compassionate and authentic inner voice. Therapy and self-reflection can be helpful in exploring and transforming these internal narratives to foster emotional growth.

The inner voice of secure attachment

Secure attachment refers to a healthy and positive emotional bond between a child and their primary caregivers, typically forming in early childhood. This attachment style influences how individuals perceive themselves and their relationships with others, including their self-talk. Here's how secure attachment can impact our self-talk:

* **Positive self-image:** Individuals with secure attachment tend to have a more positive self-image and higher self-esteem. This can lead to more positive and more self-affirming self-talk, in which they speak kindly and compassionately to themselves.

* **Trust in relationships:** Securely attached individuals feel comfortable depending on others and seeking support when needed. This sense of security can translate into more trusting and positive self-talk, as they believe in their ability to navigate challenges and setbacks.

* **Emotional regulation:** Secure attachment provides a sense of emotional security and stability, enabling individuals to regulate their emotions effectively. This can lead to healthier self-talk patterns, where individuals are better able to manage stress, anxiety and negative emotions through self-soothing and positive self-reassurance.

* **Resilience:** Securely attached individuals have a strong foundation of support and connection, which can contribute to greater resilience in the face of adversity. This resilience is reflected in their self-talk, as they are more likely to adopt a growth mindset, view setbacks as opportunities for learning and growth, and engage in problem-solving rather than self-defeating thoughts.

In summary, secure attachment fosters a positive self-image, trust in relationships, emotional regulation and resilience, all of which can impact our self-talk in a constructive and supportive way. Individuals with secure attachment are more likely to engage in positive, self-affirming and compassionate self-talk, promoting overall emotional well-being and psychological health. Secure attachment is the foundation of having not just independence but interdependence. Interdependence allows us to be emotionally vulnerable and open in relationships while at the same time allowing us to maintain a sense of self-worth that is not based on relationships. Some people have a secure attachment style because of the environment they grew up in or because of the work they did to get themselves there. Being able to bring ourselves into a secure attachment style is an incredible foundation from which we can explore the world, ourselves and others without fear of rejection and without unhealthy attachment needs.

Emotions and our inner voice

Every emotion can trigger changes in our inner voice. As emotions are naturally transient, most of these changes can be temporary and don't really impact the longer-term nature, tone and habits of our inner voice. But at times, significant emotions can be so strong and linked to critical experiences in our lives that we become stuck in these emotions. They can become a consistent part of our being and, therefore, can have a lasting impact on the very nature of our inner voice. Shame and guilt are two examples of disempowering emotions:

Shame and guilt

Guilt and shame are commonly confused emotions, but they have distinct differences in terms of their origin and impact on individuals. Guilt implies 'I have done something wrong'; shame implies 'I am wrong'.

Guilt is typically related to a specific behaviour or action that someone has taken or failed to take. It is the feeling of remorse or regret for doing something wrong or not meeting one's own standards or values. Guilt is often focused on the behaviour itself and can serve as a healthy emotional response to acknowledge and take responsibility for our actions. It can motivate us to correct our behaviour, make amends and learn from our mistakes.

Shame, on the other hand, is a more pervasive and internalised emotion that is focused on the self rather than a specific behaviour. **It is the feeling of being fundamentally flawed, unworthy or inadequate as a person.** Shame is often tied to our identity and self-worth, rather than just a specific action. Shame can be more damaging than guilt, as it can lead to feelings of worthlessness, self-criticism and a deep sense of inadequacy.

In summary, guilt is related to a specific behaviour or action, and it can motivate us to make amends and improve, while shame is more focused on our core identity and can lead to deeper feelings of inadequacy and unworthiness. It is important to distinguish between guilt and shame, as they require different responses in order to heal and move forward in a healthy way.

Shame and guilt are complex emotions that can have a significant impact on our inner voice and self-perception in several ways:

* **Negative self-talk:** When we experience shame or guilt, our inner voice may become critical and self-blaming. We may engage in negative self-talk, berating ourselves for our perceived shortcomings or mistakes. This can perpetuate feelings of unworthiness, self-doubt and self-criticism.

* **Self-judgement:** They can lead to harsh self-judgement and a sense of personal failure. Our inner voice may reinforce feelings of inadequacy, incompetence or shame, creating a cycle of self-criticism and self-condemnation.

* **Distorted beliefs:** They can distort our beliefs about ourselves and our actions. Our inner voice may perpetuate negative self-perceptions and flawed interpretations of events, reinforcing those feelings of shame, guilt and self-blame.

* **Fear of vulnerability:** They can drive us to avoid vulnerability and emotional openness. Our inner voice may discourage us from acknowledging our emotions, expressing our needs or seeking support from others out of fear of judgement, rejection or further shame.

* **Inhibition of self-expression:** They can inhibit our ability to express ourselves authentically and assert our needs. Our inner voice may silence our desires and emotions, leading to feelings of emotional suppression, disconnection and inner turmoil.

* **Difficulty connecting:** They can interfere with our relationships by influencing our inner voice to mistrust others, fear rejection or withdraw from emotional intimacy. Our inner dialogue may perpetuate a sense of unworthiness, undermining our ability to form close, healthy connections with others.

* **Self-worth:** They can erode our sense of self-worth and self-compassion. Our inner voice may reinforce feelings of shame, guilt and self-blame, undermining our confidence, self-esteem and ability to nurture a positive self-image.

Overall, shame and guilt can have a profound impact on our inner voice by fostering self-criticism, self-judgement, distorted beliefs, fear of vulnerability, inhibited self-expression and negative self-perceptions. It is important to recognise and address these emotions in a compassionate and non-judgemental way, seeking support from others, practising self-care and cultivating self-compassion to foster emotional healing and growth. Therapy, mindfulness practices and self-reflection can be valuable tools in exploring and transforming our inner dialogue to better promote self-acceptance, self-awareness and emotional well-being.

*

In my book *The Freedom Within*, I did a deep dive into human emotions – why we have them, where we experience and store them, and the impact they have on our lives and our health. I took readers through a deep exploration of the array of human emotions and came to the point that, in fact, we only have two human emotions: love and fear.

Fear shows up in so many various but connected emotions; fear disguises itself as anger, comparison, judgement, impatience, shame and guilt. While all of these emotions have nuances, they are all part of the 'fear' family. One of the ways we can get beyond the emotion of fear is by regularly and actively cultivating the emotion of love. The more we cultivate feelings of love and gratitude, the more we replace the feelings of shame, fear and guilt. The brain and nervous system will always attach to the most powerful emotion, and love is by far the most powerful emotion. The more we generate and experience love or the emotions that come out of love, the less we experience the emotions of fear. This has a massive impact on the nature and tone of our inner voice. A great starting point in generating the emotion of love is to generate gratitude. Gratitude, compassion, non-judgement and self-compassion are all in the family of love and are all examples of empowering emotions.

Gratitude

Gratitude has a profound impact on our inner voice by creating a sense of positivity, optimism and self-love. When we cultivate gratitude, we are focusing on the good in our lives and acknowledging the blessings we have. This practice helps to shift our perspective from a negative or critical inner voice to one that is more compassionate, kind and empowering.

When we express gratitude, we are acknowledging our strengths, our accomplishments and the support we have received from others. This appreciation helps to counteract negative self-talk and self-criticism, replacing it with feelings of fulfilment and contentment. As a result, our inner voice becomes more supportive, encouraging and nurturing.

Additionally, gratitude can help to improve our overall well-being by reducing stress, anxiety and depression. When we practise gratitude regularly, we are training our brains to focus on the positive aspects of our lives, which can help to boost our mood and increase our resilience in the face of challenges.

By cultivating a sense of gratitude, we can transform our inner dialogue and create a more nurturing and empowering self-talk.

Ways to practise gratitude

The first simple way to practise gratitude on a daily basis is with a gratitude journal. Choose a time of day when you have a few minutes – it only takes a short time to stop, reflect and get a new perspective. It may be first thing in the morning, during lunch, while commuting or before bedtime.

Simply think of three to five things for which you are currently grateful – from the everyday (you have food to eat, a bed to sleep in) to the magnificent (your child's first steps, the people that love you most, the beauty of the sky at night) – then write them down.

By taking time to stop and write down these things, by acknowledging them, you are bringing them into the level of conscious awareness. You are telling your nervous system that these are the things you want to focus on; these are the things you want to reconnect to. And once you begin that deliberate conscious thought, where you bring your attention and awareness to these things, your brain forgets that you are merely 'thinking' about them and actually believes that you are living those moments again. We then begin to experience the same emotions we felt when we lived these moments in real time. So, the very act of taking time to stop and bring into conscious awareness the things that you are grateful for leads you to generate the emotions of love and joy and connection from a chemical point of view.

We should never underestimate the power of writing things down. And writing down what we're grateful for gives the brain something new to focus on. It makes us take time to bring our attention to what is right and not just what is wrong. It makes us take time to remember the things that we have, which creates an abundance mindset, instead of focusing on the things we don't have, which creates a lack and limitation mindset.

An important recommendation is to keep your gratitude practice fresh by varying it and not over-practising it. If you count your blessings every single day in the exact same way, in a nonvarying routine, you might become bored, so it won't have the same impact.

Another powerful gratitude practice I use is to create a little video. My technology skills are fairly limited, so the videos I create are very simple. You can use any of the phone apps where you upload some photos and add music to them, or it can be as simple as a PowerPoint presentation, where you enable the presentation to run by itself. Either way, you have a short 'gratitude' movie that features the moments and people you are deeply grateful for.

My video features pictures of my wife and my beautiful children. Pictures of some of the funny things we've done – dancing around the house, going down a hill in a go-kart. And attached to that video is a beautiful song that says 'You are my reason.' **My family are my reason for everything. And some-times, like everybody else, I forget this.** I get too distracted by work, I get too distracted by what's going on around me, and I can forget that the things that are of greatest value and importance are right in front of me.

This simple gratitude video takes so little time, yet the combination of the slideshow and music transforms me mentally, emotionally and chemically, and brings me to a place where I feel love and joy. Even in that short period, it elevates my attention, awareness and emotion away from fear and back to love.

I even use these techniques with the greatest athletes. They can help anybody shift and change their emotions in that moment, whether it's through journaling, music or video. So let's begin by picking a gratitude practice, and for the next few weeks, make sure that it becomes a daily activity, where you take time to elevate your emotions, elevate your stories and elevate your perspective. .

Simple gratitude journaling prompts

1. Who is it that brings me most joy?
2. Where and with whom do I feel loved?
3. What does feeling this type of love feel like?
4. What is my happiest memory?
5. What in my life can I be most grateful for right now?
6. What is the characteristic that I am most proud of?
7. What three things have I experienced that I am proud of?

CHAPTER 3
PAIN STORY OR
POWER STORY?

Moving from sabotage to strength

The more we break down the various habits and patterns of our inner voice and inner narrative, the more we can simplify it and the impact it is having on every aspect of our life. We can break every habit and pattern into one of two possible outcomes:

1. Empowerment narrative
2. Disempowerment narrative

As simple as this is, it gives us a clear framework to be able to distil and identify our inner voice and inner narrative. Let's take a closer look.

The pain narrative

Ego is the author of the pain narrative. There is a close connection between the ego and our inner voice, as they both play a role in shaping our self-perception, identity and behaviour.

Most people think that 'ego' is something to do with a person who believes they are above or better than everyone else. 'Ego' is often associated with the brash and the self-absorbed, but this is not ego at all: this is simply self-centredness and obnoxiousness. Ego can be in full flight in the quietest, most reserved person you know.

Ego is the part of us that is linked to our feelings of safety and security, the part of us that clings to our past – our experiences, our memories, our traumas and our beliefs. It combines all these things to give us a label to identify with:

'I am the quiet one.'

'I am the one with no confidence.'

'I am the one who never gets a break.'

'I am the unlucky one.'

These are all labels we give ourselves, created by our ego to give us an identity that is different to everyone else's.

The ego is always consciously or subconsciously committed to supporting the thinking brain – to keep us alive, keep us protected and away from danger, whether that danger is real, remembered or imagined. In order to do this, our ego is always in a state of high alert, and it often keeps us locked in a state of anxiety, worry and fear.

We all have an ego. What differs between people is not the presence of ego but the nature and preoccupation of the ego and the work needed to regulate it. A healthy and balanced ego can actually be a powerful asset. **Our ego is not a bad part of us – it is not deliberately trying to derail us and our dreams; it is simply scared that we won't achieve them.** The ego uses self-sabotage as a self-preservation tool; it is afraid that if we try something new, if we dare to go after our dreams and we fail, we will be devastated, and the ego doesn't want us to be devastated. The ego will gladly accept current unhappiness (the familiar and safe) rather than the chance of potentially greater unhappiness if we take risks.

The angry ego fears abandonment more than anything. The ego is the part of us that is always afraid that we are not enough and that we will be left behind and abandoned. If we have had an experience of being abandoned in the past, our ego can store this memory and keep it as an active reality, which means we are always afraid of being abandoned. This is a catch-22 cycle. Because the ego is afraid of abandonment, it can make it difficult for us to have deep, meaningful relationships where we dare to give our heart and soul. The ego is so afraid you might be abandoned again that it will either find ways to prevent you from getting into these relationships or find ways to sabotage them and get you out of them before you get hurt. The ironic thing is that all these actions to prevent us from feeling abandoned actually result in us being alone, and they further reinforce our deepest fear and belief that we will be abandoned and left behind. With the best will in the world, our ego has an incredible way of creating the exact situations it fears.

The ego will fight anyone and anything that challenges this one-dimensional vision of who we are. It wants to make sure that our future self will be an extension of our past self and that we will continue to think and feel as we have in the past. The ego will trap us in untrue stories about who we are, what we can do and what we can achieve to prevent us from changing. It will very quickly dismiss anything or anyone that challenges it or risks it being exposed. If we encounter someone or something that has a different life vision, a different belief system or a different life choice, the ego will try to convince us that they are wrong. Anything other than the thoughts, beliefs and habits that match the ones of our ego will be rapidly dismissed, and we will find ourselves judging others as 'wrong' – as hippies, as ruthless business people, as religious nuts, as too young, too old. Without truly exploring these different beliefs, we dismiss them instantly.

The ego will do the same when we start to express ourselves differently. The moment we think *Maybe I could get the job*; *Maybe I could write a book*; *Maybe I could find true love*, the ego will quickly come in and dismiss the thought because it only knows you as the person you are now and the person you have always been – and that person doesn't have their dream job, has never written a book and has never found love.

The ego can influence our inner voice by filtering and interpreting our experiences, perceptions and emotions through the lens of our beliefs and values. It acts as a self-regulating mechanism that helps us maintain a coherent sense of self and navigate the complexities of our internal and external worlds. The ego can impact our inner voice by shaping our self-image, self-esteem and self-worth, leading to patterns of positive or negative self-talk based on our perceived strengths, weaknesses and insecurities.

Additionally, the ego can influence the content and tone of our inner voice by defending against threats to our self-image and identity. It may engage in defensive or protective mechanisms, such as denial, rationalisation or projection, to cope with challenges and maintain a sense of control and stability. This can result in an inner voice that is critical, judgemental or defensive, reflecting our efforts to protect our ego and maintain a sense of self-preservation.

To cultivate a healthier relationship between the ego and our inner voice, it is important to practise self-awareness, mindfulness and self-reflection. By becoming conscious of the ego's influence on our thoughts and behaviours, we can challenge and reframe negative self-talk, cultivate self-compassion and acceptance, and align our inner voice with our values, authenticity and growth. Developing a balanced and integrated sense of self can help us navigate the complexities of the ego and transform our pain narrative into a power narrative.

The power narrative

The soul is the author of the power narrative. We, at all times, have the opportunity to cultivate and develop a power narrative. In a power narrative, our inner voice uses words that uplift and inspire us. A power narrative is one that isn't focused on and caught up in your past. It focuses on opportunity, not threat – on what you do have, not what you don't have. A power narrative is the voice deep within that says, 'Come on, you got this.'

> There is freedom waiting for you
> On the breezes of the sky
> And you ask 'What if I fall?'
> Oh but my darling, what if you fly?

I come back to these beautiful lines by the poet Erin Hanson again and again in my life, especially at times when I am doubting myself, allowing my inner voice to breed fear, and my ego is asking, 'What if you fall?' Once we ask ourselves this question, we are giving our inner voice, our ego and our deepest subconscious fears licence to catastrophise, to create infinite worst-case scenarios that will ensure we avoid the opportunity. Instead, we retreat into our safe old existence, where there is no danger for now, but at some point in the future we will face the greatest of dangers – where we get to a point in our lives where we recognise that we missed out on opportunities and held ourselves back, so we are filled with regret.

I firmly believe that the greatest tragedy in life is not death: it is getting to the end and realising we never actually lived. The greatest tragedy is all the little dreams and opportunities we allow to die within us while we live.

The most important promise I have made to myself is that I will live a life with no regrets – I will give myself permission to follow my heart and follow my dreams. This means that I may very well make mistakes, I may very well fall short, and I am happy with that because falling short is not failure: failure is not pursuing, which leads to regret. Once we dare to set off on the incredible journey that our heart is calling us to embark on, we have already succeeded – we have already set ourselves free.

So, in times when I doubt myself, when I can't see the second step of the journey and I don't know how things are going to work out, I come back to those magnificent words by Erin Hanson and instead of asking myself, 'What if I fall?', I ask myself, 'What if I fly?'

The moment we change the direction and the nature of the question, we change where the answer comes from. Instead of fear and limitation, the answer comes from excitement and enthusiasm. It awakens a dream, it deactivates the ego, and it ignites our soul. **Once we dare to ask, 'What if I fly?', we are challenging and changing our inner voice and narrative from one of disempowerment, which is created by the ego, to one of empowerment, which is created by the soul.**

At every moment a power narrative is magnifying the solution, not the problem; it speaks about what is possible, not what's out of reach. At every moment, the power narrative is asking, 'What if I fly?'

Inner critic or inner coach?

Is your story driven by fear or love? When you listen to your inner voice, is it your inner critic or your inner coach? The inner critic is the spokesperson of the ego; the inner coach is the spokesperson of the soul. While both can exist, ultimately you have to choose which of these voices you are going to act on. The one that becomes the loudest, the stronger one that we hear in a pressurised environment, is the one we actively use and feed in our everyday life. **Our everyday inner voice, the words we use, the tone in which we speak to ourselves, is either building an incredibly empowering and healing inner coach or it is building a disempowering and hurtful inner critic.**

Our inner critic is the voice within us that often takes a negative or critical approach towards us. It is a part of our inner dialogue that can be harsh, judgemental and self-critical, focusing on our perceived flaws, mistakes and shortcomings.

The inner critic can be influenced by various factors, such as past experiences, societal expectations and internalised beliefs about ourselves.

The inner critic can manifest in different ways, such as:

*   **Self-blame:** The inner critic may constantly criticise and blame us for our mistakes, failures and perceived inadequacies.

*   **Perfectionism:** The inner critic may set impossibly high standards for us and criticise us harshly when we fail to meet them.

*   **Comparison:** The inner critic may constantly compare us to others, highlighting our perceived shortcomings and reinforcing feelings of inadequacy.

*   **Negative self-talk:** The inner critic may engage in negative self-talk, reinforcing self-doubt, low self-esteem and a negative self-image.

*   **Fear of failure:** The inner critic may discourage us from taking risks, trying new things or pursuing our goals out of fear of failure and criticism.

*   **Self-sabotage:** The inner critic may undermine our efforts towards self-improvement, personal growth and self-compassion, perpetuating cycles of self-defeating behaviour.

It is important to recognise and address our inner critic in a compassionate and non-judgemental way, challenging its negative messages and cultivating self-compassion and self-awareness. By becoming aware of our inner critic, we can begin to reframe our negative self-talk, practise self-acceptance and cultivate a more supportive and empowering inner dialogue.

Our inner coach is the positive and supportive voice within us that encourages, motivates and uplifts us. It is the nurturing and compassionate part of our inner dialogue that helps us build confidence, self-esteem and resilience. The inner coach serves as a source of encouragement, guidance and inspiration, helping us navigate challenges, setbacks and moments of self-doubt.

The inner coach can manifest in different ways, such as:

* **Positive self-talk:** The inner coach uses kind and affirming language to remind us of our strengths, capabilities and potential for growth.

* **Encouragement:** The inner coach offers words of encouragement and support, empowering us to take risks, overcome obstacles and pursue our goals.

* **Self-compassion:** The inner coach practises both self-compassion and self-acceptance, acknowledging our humanity and worthiness, even in the face of mistakes and imperfections.

* **Motivation:** The inner coach fuels our motivation and determination, helping us stay focused, committed and resilient in the pursuit of our aspirations.

* **Problem-solving:** The inner coach helps us approach challenges and setbacks with a positive and solution-focused mindset, encouraging us to learn from experiences and adapt to change.

Our inner critic fuels a pain narrative, while our inner coach fuels a power narrative. Perhaps your pain narrative appears at vulnerable moments, in times of friction with yourself, with others and/or with the world, even though this is when you need your power narrative the most. Perhaps your inner critic surprises you, popping up at moments of quiet to disrupt your peace of mind.

This is normal. Having an inner critic is not the problem – we all have one at certain times, perhaps even all the time. The big question is, when you have an inner critic who is loud and trying to take over the show, do you have an inner coach who is developed enough, strong enough, and has your permission to step in and override it? **Having an inner critic is not really the issue; not having an inner coach to counteract it is the problem.**

If we dial down the noise of our inner critic, our inner coach will step up for us. This is possible for everyone to achieve, but you might first need to identify the story your inner voice is narrating, the story that's getting most of your attention. If this story is disabling you, it's time to awaken your inner coach.

CHAPTER 4
WHAT'S YOUR STORY?

Identifying how you communicate yourself to the world

Now, I want to turn the focus over to you. I want to give you a simple framework to begin to understand your inner voice more deeply. To be able to do this accurately, we must be able to listen to our inner voice without judgement or comparison, as these only shut down the self-enquiry phase. All self-enquiry should be compassionate enquiry, so that we are not condemning or blaming our inner voice or ourselves. We must be willing to listen to it and meet it with curiosity, knowing that no matter what our self-talk contains right now, it's not there to deliberately hurt or restrict you; it's simply trying to keep you safe.

At the same time, don't become over-attached to or defensive about any part of your self-talk and inner voice. No matter how normal it may seem to you, it might not be normal at all, and no matter how much you feel that this is the only way you can speak to yourself, remain open to the fact that there may be an entirely different way.

So, as we work through this chapter, keep an open mind and an open heart, and have fun knowing that, as long as you approach it from a mindset of love, you can transform your inner voice into anything you want it to be.

An effective way to identify your key habits in how you communicate to yourself and others is to keep a journal of your thoughts and emotions throughout the day. Take note of the language you use when talking to yourself, and pay attention to any recurring negative or self-critical patterns.

Recurring self-critical patterns

'I'm not very good at ...'/'I'm not as good as ...'

_____

_____

_____

_____

_____

_____

Next, reflect on the situations or triggers that tend to bring out your inner critic. Ask yourself what specific thoughts or beliefs are at the root of these patterns, and consider how they may be impacting your self-esteem and confidence.

Trigger

You got some challenging feedback.

Root

An overly critical parent.

_____   _____

_____   _____

_____   _____

_____   _____

I AM. I CAN. I WILL.

Once you have identified these key habits, challenge yourself to reframe and shift your internal dialogue towards a more positive and empowering perspective. Remember to practise self-compassion and remind yourself that you are worthy of love and respect.

Inner critic dialogue	Inner coach dialogue
I'm not good enough,	*That's difficult feedback*
I'll never get a break.	*but also an incredible*
	opportunity for growth.

Now, let's look at how you communicate with others. Think of a time when you found yourself in the following situations:

* When people have let you down.

* When people have said they were going to do something for you and then they didn't.

* When people pull out of something you have arranged at the last moment without a really valid excuse.

* When you go over and above for others, but when you need them to do something for you, they don't.

* When your boundaries haven't been respected.

* When people have treated you in a way that was not aligned with your values and not aligned with the person you want to be.

* When somebody has treated you in a way that was unacceptable.

Choose one situation you have experienced and write about it here:

Situation

_____

_____

_____

_____

_____

Now, think about your reaction in those moments, how you felt and acted:

* What was your communication?

* Did you speak openly and honestly?

* Did you downplay your hurt and disappointment?

* Did you challenge any excuses?

* What is the consequence of your communication in that way, for them and for yourself?

Take the situation you wrote about above and record your reaction here:

Reaction

_____

_____

_____

_____

_____

Ask yourself the following questions:

* When I feel my boundaries are not respected, do I have the courage and confidence to communicate that with clarity and certainty?

* When I feel that somebody is not treating me with the respect I deserve, can I quickly and easily bring that to their attention and insist that in order to engage with me, this must change?

* When somebody has promised me that they will do something and then at the last moment, for no real reason, they pull out, am I comfortable letting them know that I am disappointed?

* When I communicate myself to the outside world, do I intentionally use words that allow people to know that I am a serious human being with values that are important and that I am comfortable making sure that I am treated in a respectful way?

Now ask yourself:

* Do I sometimes say 'yes' when I would prefer to say 'no'?

* Do I, at times, say it doesn't matter when really it does?

* When somebody hurts me or lets me down and they make an apology that's not acceptable, do I say it's okay even when my heart tells me it's not?

* When I inhibit my truth, when I use shrinking language, when I play small, what am I prioritising? What am I not prioritising?

* When I find myself in conversations that don't inspire and uplift me, or conversations that are negative, judgemental or critical, do I have the courage, confidence and ability to say, 'This is not a conversation I am choosing to have – I am removing myself from this conversation'? Or do I sometimes get pulled into conversations that I feel I must agree with or participate in, conversations that deep down I know are not the ones I want to be having, conversations that are not fair, not honest?

Use what you've learned so far to get to the root cause of why this is. You can write it down here:

_____

_____

_____

_____

_____

If you were to write down five common things you say that shrink your presence, shrink your importance, shrink your values, shrink how seriously the world is taking you, what would they be?

1. _____
2. _____
3. _____
4. _____
5. _____

Now let's look at the opposite.

If you were a courageous speaker, if you communicated with clarity and authenticity, if you were not afraid to communicate your true magnificent being, what five statements or words would you use, both internally and externally? For example, 'I am courageous, intelligent and adaptable. I can rise to any challenge.'

Write down the five new statements that will become a hallmark of how you communicate yourself to the world.

1. _____
2. _____
3. _____
4. _____
5. _____

Now that you know what those five new empowering statements are, now that you know how you want to start communicating yourself to the world, ask yourself the most important question – a beautiful question and one of the most magnificent coaching questions there is: **What would set you free?**

What would set you free to become a clear, open, honest communicator who no longer shrinks themselves but who amplifies themselves, who demands that they're taken seriously and treated with respect?

What would set you free to become a communicator who inspires and uplifts not just yourself but also the people around you?

_____

_____

_____

_____

_____

It starts today.

No more playing small, no more shrinking, no more hiding away, no more saying one thing and meaning another. Listen to your heart, speak your truth and speak your magnificence, importance and worth into existence.

It is time to become a powerful communicator of your desires and needs.

TIME TO DO SOME WORK

Practical exercise: Self-reflection

Here's a self-reflection exercise to help you identify and understand the habits and patterns of your inner voice and self-talk.

1. Awareness and observation

Spend one week observing your self-talk. Carry your journal or use your phone to jot down instances of your self-talk throughout the day. Pay attention to:

* What you say to yourself in moments of stress

* How you talk to yourself when you accomplish something

* Your inner dialogue when you make a mistake or face criticism

2. Pattern identification

At the end of the week, review your notes.

Identify and categorise recurring themes or patterns, such as:

* Positive vs. negative self-talk

* Encouraging vs. discouraging statements

* Rational vs. irrational thoughts

* Determine common triggers that influence your self-talk (for example, specific situations, people or emotions).

3. Reflect on impact

Evaluate and reflect on how your self-talk impacts your feelings, decisions and actions. Consider questions like:

* How does positive self-talk make me feel? What actions does it lead to?

* How does negative self-talk affect my confidence and behaviour?

4. Connect to outcomes

Identify specific outcomes influenced by your self-talk. For example, did positive self-talk help you stay calm under pressure, or did negative self-talk lead to avoidance or procrastination?

5. Challenge negative self-talk

Identify negative patterns by reviewing the negative self-talk examples you've recorded.

Practise reframing negative statements into more constructive, realistic or positive ones.

For example:

Negative: 'I'll never be good at this.'

Reframed: 'I'm still learning, and with practice, I can improve.'

6. Use evidence

Find evidence to support the positive reframing. Reflect on past successes or strengths that contradict negative self-talk.

7. Foster positive self-talk

Develop a set of affirmations or positive statements that resonate with you. Use these daily to reinforce positive thinking.

8. Be kind to yourself

Practise self-compassion. When faced with setbacks, talk to yourself as you would to a friend you care for.

9. Practise gratitude

Regularly acknowledge and appreciate your accomplishments and strengths. This can shift your focus to what you're doing well rather than fixating on perceived flaws.

10. Create an action plan

Based on your reflections, set specific goals for improving your self-talk. For example, commit to catching yourself when you engage in negative self-talk and immediately reframing it.

Self-talk patterns don't change overnight. Regular reflection and conscious effort are essential. Make this exercise a part of your routine, adjusting as you gain more insights into how your inner voice influences your life.

Remember, the goal is not to eliminate all negative self-talk but to cultivate a more balanced, supportive and constructive inner dialogue that empowers you to navigate life's challenges more effectively.

Meditation

A meditation to help silence our inner critic

An audio recording in which I guide you through this meditation can be accessed on my website https://www.gerry hussey.ie/i-am-i-can-i-will-meditations with the password IAMICANIWILL.

Sit in a comfortable position with your spine straight and your palms facing up on your lap. Close your eyes and take a few deep breaths to centre yourself.

Now, bring your awareness to your inner critic. Notice the thoughts and feelings that arise when your inner critic is active. Without judgement, simply observe these thoughts and feelings.

As you continue to breathe deeply, begin to repeat the following mantra silently or out loud: 'I am not my thoughts. I release self-criticism and embrace self-love. I am worthy of compassion and kindness.'

With each repetition of the mantra, imagine a bright light shining within you, radiating love and acceptance. Visualise this light enveloping your inner critic, soothing its voice and replacing it with gentle and loving words.

Repeat the following affirmations silently or out loud: 'I am worthy of love and kindness. I release self-doubt and embrace self-empowerment. I trust in my abilities and believe in my potential.'

Continue to breathe deeply and focus on the calming light surrounding you. With each breath, feel the grip of your inner critic loosening and allow yourself to bask in the empowering energy of the light. Feel the warmth and comfort of this light as it surrounds you, and the sense of peace and calm as the grip of your inner critic loosens and fades away.

Continue to repeat the mantra and bask in the loving energy of the light for as long as you need. When you feel ready, slowly open your eyes and continue to carry this sense of self-compassion and self-love with you throughout your day. Remember that you are deserving of kindness and acceptance, and that you have the power to silence your inner critic with love and compassion.

Summary of Section 1: I Am

* You create your inner voice, so you have the power to change it.

* Your inner voice can impact much more than your mental health; it can also run riot in your nervous system.

* Choose a power story, not a pain story.

* Paying attention to how you talk to yourself is the first step towards change.

SECTION 1:

I AM

SECTION 2:

I CAN

SECTION 3:

I WILL

CHAPTER 5
SUCCESS STORIES

Write the story you tell yourself and others

A building cannot stand outside the size of its foundations, and our lives cannot be bigger or better than the size of our inner beliefs. But we can rebuild those foundations, we can renovate our self-talk, we can open ourselves up to greater possibilities.

Hopefully, by now, you are getting to a deeper under-standing of what the habits and patterns of your self-talk are, where and when you first started telling yourself that story and when you first heard that voice. I also hope that by now, you are aware of the massive impact your inner narrative is having on every aspect of your life.

No matter what you have uncovered, no matter what your inner voice is, and no matter what it has created or shaped in your life, the great news is that:

You CAN change.

You CAN let go of the past.

You CAN completely transform your inner voice.

You CAN change the soundtrack of your life.
You CAN dance to a whole new tune.

Just as we have learned that most of our current self talk is created, it is also absolutely possible that we can reshape it, change it and reprogram it. Our inner narrative is not set in stone; it is not an unmovable entity. We get to change it at any moment we choose.

In fact, from years of changing my own inner voice and my own inner narrative and helping endless clients to change theirs, I know that changing our inner narrative is a powerful step to changing our entire being. And when we change our inner narrative, we are now listening to a whole new soundtrack of life. When we are driven by a whole new set of words, when we change the tone and the nature of our inner voice, it impacts every single facet of our lives.

Only when we develop the simple tools that allow us to let the outer world dissolve and disappear can we begin to go within and hear the stories, the commentary or the emptiness that is playing within.

In order to change the record, we first need to find out how we can scratch it.

What keeps us trapped?

All transformation requires two powerful elements, which you can discover by answering these questions:

1. What new realities are you willing to open yourself up to and take on?

2. What are you willing to let go?

For me, the greatest and deepest change is only allowed to happen when we make a firm promise to release ourselves from the past, from old ways of acting and old ways of thinking. This can be a very scary process. A snake has to regularly shed its skin in order to grow and evolve. The snake is asked to let go of the thing that has kept them safe and protected for so long. If they don't, the constrictions of the old skin will prevent the snake from growing and thriving and will eventually kill it. Once the old skin is shed, the snake has to wait a while for the new skin to develop, and during this period, the snake is vulnerable. But as scary as it is, the snake knows that it has outgrown its old skin – it knows the old skin is no longer fit for purpose and that vulnerability is the key to growth and evolution.

Just like the snake, when we start to let go of the old, when we start to release all of our old defensive, protective mechanisms, we can feel vulnerable, and this is what prevents most people from continuing to change. This is why most people fall back into the safe and familiar and get stuck.

When we are scared, we must look at ourselves in the mirror and say, 'I can'. It is at these fearful moments that we face our inner stories and fears in order to release the old and take on the new. The changes won't always be immediate, and they may not always be easy, but the easy life is often the life of staying stuck, staying afraid, retreating from your dreams and ending up with regrets. Committing to change your life can be hard, but for me, no matter how hard it is, it is easier than living a lifetime in fear and ending up with a million missed opportunities.

Sometimes, we just have to choose our hard and choose the one that leads to the greatest freedom.

So, let's take a deeper look at how we actually begin to transform and how we can change our deepest beliefs and inner narrative. Below, I share some success stories of clients I work with to show you that it is entirely possible to transform your life, or an aspect of your life, using your inner voice. Keep in mind that I am only sharing what I know is necessary. I am sharing what I have experienced and witnessed when, at a pivotal moment, my client was willing to tell themselves a different story – one of passion, accountability, resilience and empowerment. A story that starts with I CAN.

Now that you have identified what you want to change, write down the pattern you are working on and we will transform it over the next few chapters.

_____

_____

_____

_____

The golfer: what are you really afraid of?

I work with a client who is a very successful golfer, which is a little strange given I have never played a single round of golf in my life. So, when I was initially asked to work with him, I was concerned that I might not be able to help him. I shared this concern with his agent and their response put me at ease: 'Gerry, this guy knows golf – there is nothing about it he doesn't know. He doesn't need someone to talk to him about golf: he needs someone to help him with the stuff that is stopping him from playing golf at the level he can.'

When I first started working with the golfer, one of the issues he had was his performance on the putting green. To make even simple putts in pressurised environments had become an issue.

When we first met, I asked him to tell me what he felt was behind this. He thought about the moments and tournaments where the pressure seemed to build and his ability to focus and execute evaporated, and as a result, he had rushed the shot, over-hit the shot, or under-hit the shot. He had abandoned his process and second-guessed himself.

We identified that in these moments, he felt pressure, and this pressure was a distraction. It took him away from a feeling of balance and focus. It took him out of a feeling of flow.

When I asked him where this pressure came from, his initial answer was the crowds and the expectations of his coaches. He believed that a lot of the pressure came from the fact that so many people watched him play week in and week out and that so many people had opinions about him. He believed that everyone was waiting to slate him. He felt that his pressure was coming from external sources.

After we chatted about this, I reminded him that pressure has nothing to do with external situations. Pressure does not come from our job or from the media. Pressure does not come from people's expectations or laws. Pressure is a physiological and chemical response that happens within us when we think about the media, when we think about other people. Pressure is an internal response that has more to do with our *thinking* about the outer world than it is to actually do with the outer world.

The first challenge to the player was to take ownership of his response. Every single tournament he played in came with an expectation of him. That is not something he could control. But his interpretation, his reaction to those expectations, was absolutely in his control.

Then we took the conversation a little bit deeper. I asked him when he was standing on those greens, in the moments where he was about to take an important putt, where was the pressure coming from?

His first response was 'I'm afraid of missing the putt. I'm afraid of letting another opportunity slip. I'm afraid of failure.'

That sounds logical for a player who desperately wants to win, but I pushed him a bit further. I asked the same question in a different way. I reminded him that golf is a beautiful game, but it's just a game, and whether that ball goes into the hole or not, nobody dies, the world isn't changed, most of the world is not watching, and most of the world doesn't care.

So I asked him who deeply cared. Who was impacting how he felt after he missed? I asked him, 'Are you afraid of missing the hole, or are you afraid of the voice that will be triggered within you when you miss the hole?'

He sat for a moment and thought about it, and then the answer became abundantly clear. He wasn't afraid of missing a shot: he was afraid of the voice that would be triggered within him if he missed – the self-anger, the hatred, the voice that says you're not good enough, and the emotions of anger, frustration and rejection that followed.

This was his realisation. What he feared had nothing to do with golf. What he feared was an inner voice that needed to be eliminated.

Once he had this new perspective, once he realised that his biggest opponent on the golf course was not the green, not the hole, not the other competitors or the spectators, but his inner voice, he saw that it was an opponent he could actually work on taking control of.

Over the months and years that followed, we worked not on his golf but on his deepest beliefs. We transformed both his beliefs and his voice, and when we did, we transformed his performance on the golf course. He now plays with freedom and joy.

My role as a performance psychologist is not necessarily to give my athletes any secret weapon or secret tool. My job is to simply take away anything that is distracting from their real performance levels. More often than not, with all the different athletes I've worked with across all the different sports I've been involved with, the consistent theme is that the greatest opponent we face is the one within. Once we dissolve this inner opponent, there are no other opponents we need to fear.

I believe that there is no such thing as a fear of failure and that nobody is afraid of the unknown. I believe what we are really afraid of is the voice that will be triggered within us by ourselves and the emotions that will follow when we fail.

When we begin to develop an inner voice that's more aligned to our inner coach, even after we fail, it will tell us, 'Let it go, it's only a shot. Let's start again, let's be brave.' **When we develop this inner coach, we fear failure less. So, ask yourself: is it failure you fear, or is it the voice in your head that will be triggered if you fail? Is it failure you fear, or is it the emotions you will feel if you fail?**

Each and every one of us gets an opportunity to develop an inner voice that is kind, loving and full of self-compassion. An inner voice that is not connected to or defined by the outcome, but one that rewards us for having the courage and bravery to pursue our dreams in the first place.

When we have an inner voice that says, 'I am, I can, I will', regardless of the outcome, we never fear failure. We will always take the chance. We will always back ourselves.

The boxer: be careful which part of the story you are paying attention to

I was working with a high-profile boxer. We were planning the next number of years, which would include international championships. As his performance psychologist, I was working with him to develop a mindset that would help him navigate the challenges and setbacks that professional sport brings. We were mapping out the various tournaments that would be the key pillars along the next few years of his journey, breaking each year into monthly targets, each month into weekly targets, and each week into daily targets.

We made sure that each day, each week, we were working on what was controllable, what was right in front of us, and that each day we were turning up with the right mindset, thinking the right way, and that we were beginning to act and feel as if we had already achieved our goals. One of the big goals this young athlete had was to become a champion in his division. During a session, we began to think about what that would look like. I asked him to close his eyes and think about what type of person would be able to win that tournament and what type of mindset that person would be required to have. If he was already a champion, how would he talk? How would he speak? How would he train?

As we know well, life doesn't always give us what we want; sometimes, life gives us who we are. So, we made a mission to start living, thinking and training as if he had already become a champion. We created visualisations and meditations that he would listen to every day, repeating the phrase 'I am a champion'. We repeated these affirmations and these visualisations over and over again. We became so emotionally connected to this future truth that it was like it had already happened.

Then we created a simple mantra: 'It is already written.' We believed, with all our hearts and souls, that the path was set, and as long as we turned up every day with the right mindset, training the right way, and doing everything we could, things would unfold exactly as they should. This athlete started telling everybody that he was going to become world champion. He spoke with clarity and focus, and when he told people he was going to become a champion, there was a truth in his eyes. It was like he was already predicting the future. Some people were sceptical. Some people said this put too much pressure on him. But it felt right. He believed what he was saying. He told himself and the world, 'I'm going to become a champion', and every day we repeated the mantra: 'It is already written.'

Eighteen months later, he was in an international championship. He was in the final, and in the first round of this fight, everything went wrong; from his tactics to his opponent, it seemed like nothing was going right. Yet, at the end of the first round, he walked back to the corner with a smile on his face, calm and relaxed. At that moment, despite having no external evidence to suggest that he was going to win the fight, everything within him, every story, every thought, every emotion was still repeating: 'I am going to win. It is already written.' Because we had focused and worked so much on the idea that the right person with the right process never worries about the outcome, at the end of the first round, full of confidence and self-belief and trusting the universe, trusting the process, he simply asked, 'What in the process do I need to change?' And in the 60 seconds between rounds, because of his calm and clear mindset, he and the coach made some simple process changes.

The bell rang. He walked back for the second round with a smile on his face, shoulders relaxed. Slowly, he began to change the process. Little things, little tweaks, now began to pay off, and the momentum began to shift. At the end of the second round, he walked back to the corner, the scores level, and there was still a smile on his face. He was now more certain than ever. He knew the momentum was changing. He knew his story was coming true.

He walked back out to the third round, and at the end of it, his arm was raised in victory.

Had he not developed that strong inner voice, had he not developed that inner mantra, maybe he would have accepted a silver medal. Maybe he would have accepted a different story. But even in that pressurised environment, his brain had one story. There was only one neurological pathway alive, and that was the one that said, 'I am, I can, I will.'

The right person with the right story never veers away from the truth. So, what is your future truth? What is your championship? What's never been done that you're going to do? What is the new mantra that you want to start speaking? When will you stop using the words 'might', 'could', 'should' and 'try' and start saying 'I can' and 'I will'?

Let's start building that mantra. Let's start building that story. The stories we tell ourselves are the seeds from which the flowers of tomorrow grow. When we are in a pressurised situation, when we are faced with a challenge, it is our deepest story, the one we have told ourselves most often, that's going to direct our energy, attention and thoughts. And that which directs our energy, awareness and attention is that which manifests the outcome. It is time to begin to tell yourself a powerful future truth about what you will do. It is time to build that story and repeat it over and over and over again until you *become* that story.

What will you do? Who will you become? It starts today.

The entrepreneur: don't let success go to your head; don't let setbacks go to your heart

I have a client who has built a very successful business and a very successful global brand. As with most successful business people, her success is based on years of dedication, commitment, resilience, self-belief and having the ability to continually rise above the noise and stay focused on her dreams, even when it seemed at times no one else believed in them.

When I first met her, she was facing so many roadblocks. There were challenges in trying to develop the product, trying to secure financing, trying to get people to believe in her vision. For the first few years, she was met with setback after setback. Finally, coming to the end of 2019, things began to shift – there was a tiny glimmer of light. But no sooner had this tiny glimmer of light appeared than it was extinguished overnight. After years of sacrifice and struggle and uncertainty, just as the business was about to explode, Covid happened, and the world shut down. As the world went into lockdown, investors pulled out, and it seemed that the business was destined for failure.

It so easily could have failed, except for one thing: the incredible mindset of this woman, a mindset of focus, passion, resilience and creativity, a mindset that embraced all challenges and welcomed all obstacles, a mindset built around a simple but powerful mantra.

Over the first few weeks of lockdown, I had a meeting with her. She was the head of the business, and given the challenges the business was now facing, she needed to be at her very best. She knew that over the next months and years, she would need to be in a better mind space than ever before.

The easy option was to accept defeat. The easy option was to accept failure. The easy option was to create an inner story of 'bad luck' and 'poor me'. But this incredible lady refused to bow to failure; she refused to bow to excuses.

So, at the beginning of Covid, she made a solemn promise that she would do everything in her power to realise her dream, and she asked me to help her develop a mindset that would enable her to be resilient and focused, knowing that she was now in one of the most challenging business environments in recent history, knowing that over the next few months, and possibly years, she would face incredible challenges.

As we spoke about how she would develop a winning mindset and how she would keep her thoughts, emotions and energy in a state of focus and manifestation, we developed a simple but powerful line that she would repeat – three simple words to say when she experienced a setback or rejection: 'for the better'.

Every rejection is a redirection. This is something I sincerely believe. When we believe in a higher power, when we believe in the universe, when we believe in ourselves, a rejection can be redirection to somewhere else, somewhere better, somewhere more powerful.

When something that you don't want or don't expect happens, say 'for the better' and it will redirect your focus and attention. A simple mantra like 'for the better' builds a sense of belief; it builds a sense of motivation.

Every single one of us will meet challenges and setbacks – be it in business or in life, a door will close on us. We could see those moments as rejections and begin to build a story in our heads that says, 'I'm not enough, life is too hard, maybe this won't work, maybe I should give up'. Then this leads to emotional depletion, eroding self-confidence, passion and our sense of enthusiasm and hope.

If, however, we see these moments not as rejections but as redirections, it builds a totally different story with a different emotional response. **When we use the mantra 'for the better', we see everything as an opportunity, not a threat.**

Over the past few years, this entrepreneur has repeatedly experienced setbacks and obstacles, but her self-belief has remained steadfast, and she has never allowed herself to give up on her dream. She took every rejection as a redirection and every door that closed as an opportunity to enhance her pitch, her process and her methods. I'm delighted to say her business has now evolved and exploded into a hugely successful global brand, and she is still using the same mindset to take her business from strength to strength.

We know now that sometimes our inner narrative is self-created and that it is often influenced by external forces. Very often, our inner voice is shaped by the people who surround us. If a narrative is repeated enough times externally, we accept it as the truth simply because so many people we have assigned power and authority to are repeating it. We then start to repeat these narratives so often that we see them as our own.

Don't sacrifice your truth to be part of the tribe

In my second book, *The Freedom Within*, I spoke about the deep and innate drive in human beings to be part of a tribe and the benefits and consequences that this drive to be part of a tribe can have. On close examination, we can discover that many of the patterns and habits of our inner voice are ones we have inherited from those who represent important attachment figures in our lives. We can often have an inner narrative that we have developed as part of a mechanism to make us and keep us as a valued member of a tribe.

At the very beginning, when humans evolved on Earth, they faced many dangers. So, in order for us to thrive and succeed, in order for us to survive, we had a better chance when we were together in numbers. In order to stay in a tribe, we had to be loved by the tribe, we had to be needed by the tribe, and therefore, it was important that we held the same belief systems as the tribe. If the tribe felt that it didn't need us or love us, if we showed a weakness or if the tribe thought we didn't have value or worth, we were left behind, which must have been a terrifying place to be. Having a different belief system could be a dangerous thing, as social acceptance was more important than self-expression, and so people took on the beliefs of the tribe and perhaps never even questioned them – we were in the pursuit of fitting in, not in pursuit of the truth.

This is still part of the human psyche and why, at times, we are afraid to show vulnerability. We are afraid if we don't have value, if we don't have a contribution to make, if we're not loved or needed, we will be left behind. Accepting the tribe's beliefs is a way of ensuring this doesn't happen.

'Groupthink' is a phenomenon that occurs within a group of people when the desire for harmony or conformity in the group results in irrational or dysfunctional decision-making. It can significantly influence our inner voice by shaping our beliefs, values and perceptions based on the predominant opinions of the group. When we are surrounded by a group of like-minded individuals, we might feel pressured to conform to the group mentality. This can lead to a suppression of our own authentic voice and independent thinking, as we prioritise fitting in with the group over expressing our true thoughts and feelings.

Furthermore, groupthink can create a sense of cognitive bias, where we might ignore or dismiss dissenting viewpoints in favour of maintaining harmony. This can result in a narrowing of our perspective and limit our ability to critically evaluate information or make independent decisions.

Key characteristics of groupthink include:

* **Illusion of invulnerability:** Group members believe they are invincible and can do no wrong, leading to a false sense of confidence in their decisions.

* **Rationalisation:** Members may ignore or rationalise any warning signs or alternative viewpoints that contradict the group's beliefs.

* **Stereotyping:** Outsiders or dissenters may be stereotyped or belittled to maintain the group's cohesion.

* **Pressure of conformity:** Those who express dissenting opinions may face pressure to conform to the group's consensus.

* **Self-censorship:** Members might hesitate to express their true thoughts or feelings due to fear of rejection or criticism from the group.

* **Illusion of unanimity:** There is a perception that everyone in the group is in agreement, even if there are underlying doubts or concerns.

Overall, groupthink can hinder critical thinking, creativity and the ability to consider alternative perspectives, ultimately leading to flawed decision-making processes. It is important to be aware of the pitfalls of groupthink and strive to foster an environment that values diversity of thought and encourages open and honest communication within groups.

In essence, the impact of groupthink on our inner voice can be profound, as it can influence the way we perceive ourselves, others and the world around us. Being mindful of the potential effects of groupthink and striving to maintain our individuality and independent thought processes in order to cultivate a strong and authentic inner voice is essential.

The following story is a simple and practical yet powerful real-life example of how fast the masses can absorb a narrative through groupthink.

Don't be afraid to jump: Lessons from the Forty Foot

It is a beautiful Friday morning, and I'm making my way to the Forty Foot in Sandycove, Dublin, as is my normal Friday morning routine. The Forty Foot is a beautiful, deep little cove where you can swim in the ocean. I'm not sure whether it's the cold-water immersion in the Atlantic or the warmth of a cup of tea and a chat with friends afterwards that contains the magic. All I know is that if you put them both together, you have a magic morning in store.

Anyone who is familiar with the Forty Foot knows there is a rock that makes a great diving spot, and when the tide is in, or in just enough, it gives like-minded adventurers a chance to let their inner child out to play and dive from the rock into the water. It's not a very big jump; it's just big enough to give you a nice bit of excitement and a small adrenaline rush.

On this particular Friday morning, I'm excited and ready for my jump. I put my togs on and make my way to the rock. When I get to the top, there's a number of people standing there, looking down, but no one is jumping.

'Is there something wrong?' I asked.

'No,' they said, 'it's just too low. We were going to jump but the water is not deep enough.'

I'm no expert in marine science, but as a regular visitor to this area, I looked at the water and everything inside of me said that the water was high enough. But these guys looked fairly certain; there was confidence in their voices. So, I took a moment and waited.

As I was waiting, a number of other people came up ready and excited to jump in, but once they saw the crowd, they asked the same question I had and got the same answer. 'The water isn't high enough. It's too low.'

I was still looking at the water level. Although I had listened to the story that it was too low, and I could hear confidence in the voices of the people saying it and those repeating it, it didn't make sense. I knew in my heart that the water was more than deep enough to jump in.

I turned to tell the group that I was going to jump, but there was nobody there. They had all left. They had all retreated back down the rock.

Here goes, I thought to myself, *it's now or never.*

I took a deep breath and jumped. Seconds later I hit the water with a splash and, of course, the water was more than deep enough – it always was.

Sometimes we retreat from the rock not because the water level is too low, but because our self-doubt is too high.

What happened was that one person, either based on lack of evidence, lack of knowledge or lack of courage, decided the jump wasn't for them, and to justify their own decision, perhaps to camouflage their own fear and self-doubt, they created a story. But because they told that story with such confidence, people bought into it. That person did not retreat from the rock because the water level was too low: he retreated from the rock because his self-doubt was too high; but the story of self-doubt is a difficult one to tell so he told the story about the water level, as that was easier.

This is the problem with groupthink: intelligent, clever people will often and easily be convinced of a story, despite not taking the time to fact-check it themselves. We can often use this external story to dismiss our internal truth.

It's important that we listen to what the masses are saying. It's also important that we challenge it.

Where's the fact? Where's the science coming from? Why

are they saying this? When we begin to apply critical thinking, we begin to realise that, very often, just because the masses are saying something doesn't make it true. Groupthink can be a major factor in shaping our inner self-talk, our inner narrative and our communication styles. But we must be careful of the stories we buy into.

This next story shows how narratives of the masses not only can often be incorrect, but also might have been consciously or unconsciously created to support one person's agenda.

Don't buy into shitty stories

Over the last few years, I have been fortunate to work with an amazing guy called Mike Thomas. Mike works as an Alpine guide, leading individuals and teams up some of the most incredible mountains in the world. He is one of the most impressive human beings and one of the most impressive leaders I have ever come across. He has an incredible way of guiding people through even the most challenging and dangerous environments.

But as a leader, above all, he makes his team feel safe and cared for, and he inspires them and gives them courage that they would not have without him. He is very selective with the words he uses, and he is extremely careful about the stories he allows himself or anybody in the expedition to tell. While always adhering to safety protocols, he empowers his team to look at the possibility, to look at the potential and to focus on where they have control, breaking even the biggest mountains down into achievable pieces.

Many times, just when there's a story of fatigue or fear building – that maybe we won't get to the summit, it's too high, the climb's too hard – or a story of complacency emerges, which is equally destructive, Mike would listen to the story and carefully, without dismissing it, place another story in our heads. He would say, 'How about we just get to the next rock?', 'Why don't we just go and have a look?', or 'How about we think about it for twenty minutes and reassess then?' Mike listens to everybody's story, without dismissing it, but then he challenges us with a better story.

It is very important that Mike regulates the words and language he uses. He selects words and questions that empower and uplift, while at the same time acknowledging the risk and danger that can be part and parcel of climbing mountains, just like they are in life.

On one occasion, I was asking Mike how he knows when to push and go on and how he knows when it's time to go back down the mountain. It's a difficult call to make. He gave me many incredible insights, but one story really struck me. He described a scenario where you are guiding a team up a mountain and you happen to meet a team on the way down, and the descending team have abandoned the climb, having decided that it is too risky, that the mountain is too high. They have decided it is impossible.

Mike said that at that moment it's important to ask the right questions. The right questions are simply about acknowledging the terrain and identifying if something unforeseen has happened above. Otherwise, communication with that other team should be kept to a minimum. When I asked him why, he explained that the descending team have made the decision to abandon the climb and they want to justify that decision. In order to justify that decision, they will try to convince everybody else that the decision was right.

He said, if we engage with them long enough, they might convince us that the mountain is too high, so that we, too, abandon our journey and our dreams.

Mike has met many teams on their way down, having abandoned the mountain, but Mike has kept his own team going, and they have successfully navigated to the top. It was a simple yet eye-opening story that shows the power of trusting yourself and your instincts. It also highlights the danger of asking too many people for advice and opinions. People can only tell you what is possible for them. People can only see a mountain or a life through the lens of their own story and their own beliefs, and they will try to force those stories and beliefs on you to justify their decisions and actions.

After telling me that story, as we walked along, Mike could tell that I was really thinking about it, so he smiled and said, 'Gerry, I have an expression I think you will like. It's a little bit rude but I think you will get it. Shitty people with shitty beliefs tell themselves and others shitty stories to justify their shitty decisions and shitty actions.'

Be careful who you ask for opinions and facts, for at best they can only give you an opinion that is true for them, and even their 'facts' can be altered and manipulated by their deepest needs and beliefs. **Know that you can tune into your inner voice and dial down the noise of the tribe, the group-think and external group fear.** When you do, what's left is the truth – your truth, and that is the most important and accurate truth there is. It will never be wrong. When we are equipped and empowered by our truth, we can summit mountains – not just real mountains, but the mountains of our biggest dreams.

CHAPTER 6
SCRATCH THE RECORD

How you can disrupt the narrative and change the truth

The alarm sounds. It's 5.30 a.m., I've been asleep for only two hours, and it's time to get up.

We have two young kids who have been in the bed with us all night and, for some reason, on this particular night, they have decided that they would spend most of it awake, singing, dancing, laughing, crying, screaming and generally jumping around the room creating chaos. For anybody who has stayed in a hotel room with two young kids, you will know it can be quite an adventure, and this night we had the adventure of a lifetime.

On most days, this wouldn't be a major issue, as at some point throughout the day we might get a chance to stop, breathe and recover.

But this day is different for me.

Today, I will have a thousand people arriving in the National Concert Hall in Dublin for an event that I put on once a year, an event where I bring passion and joy and energy

... and where I will be standing on stage for over six hours, delivering content and meditations. It is a day, as you can imagine, that requires a calm focus and a huge amount of energy. It's a day in preparation for which I would have hoped to have had at least some sleep the night before.

As I wake at 5.30 in the morning, the first story that enters my head is that I'm tired. The second story is that we should have done this differently. Maybe I should have stayed in my own room; maybe we should have had the kids stay somewhere else – these are all the 'should haves' that are running through my mind. As I keep focusing on the things that are wrong, my story turns to anger.

Very quickly, this negativity spirals, and it evolves into a story that I'm not just tired, but I'm *too* tired. How can I deliver on a big day like today? How will I be able to perform?

That negative question leads to a negative answer: 'I won't be able to. I'll be tired. I'll be flat. This isn't fair.' The story gives rise to a vision of a tired me standing on the stage, not knowing what to say, delivering a flat performance and having an audience of a thousand flat people.

At that moment, I know something has to change. We have invested far too much time and energy into this event. People have bought tickets and are already travelling to the venue. I have a decision to make: either call off the event or call off my negative self-talk.

It is now time to scratch the record. It is now time to change the truth.

So instead of engaging with this conversation any longer, I decide the event is going ahead. It is going to be magnificent, the people who attend it will be magnificent, and today will be a magnificent day.

I'm trying to tell myself this story, but my body isn't yet feeling it. My nervous system is still screaming exhaustion. My eyes are beginning to close. So, I decide that lying in bed and telling myself a story is not enough. I get out of bed, put my runners, shorts and T-shirt on, and I leave the room as quietly as possible, trying not to wake my children and my wife. I head downstairs to the gym. It's 5.45 a.m. and it's nice and quiet. I select some music that's going to uplift me and remind me that life isn't always straightforward. We don't always get the preparation we think we will, but we can always choose our response.

And now I have to choose my response. It isn't enough to tell myself a story: I have to engage my nervous system as well. I have to make sure that every cell in my body is responding to the story that this is going to be a magnificent day. I need endorphins. I need oxytocin. So it's time to go.

After a gentle warm-up, I get on the treadmill. As I'm running, I start to breathe deeply, and I notice a mirror in front of me. Looking at myself in the mirror, I forget the treadmill – I just keep running and watching and observing. Suddenly I begin to speak to the person looking back at me in the mirror. I start to ask them, 'Do you know who you are? Have you forgotten who you are?' I start to tell that person, 'You're amazing. You're incredible.' I start to say, 'Let's go, champ. Let's go, champ.'

At 5.50 in the morning, I'm on a treadmill in a hotel, looking at myself in a mirror, and I'm screaming, 'LET'S GO, CHAMP.' If anybody had seen me, they would have thought, *That guy's insane*, but there's a beautiful expression that goes 'And those who were dancing were thought to be insane by those who could not hear the music.' I was beginning to hear the music. I was beginning to hear a new song. I was beginning to feel my body come alive. As I ran and I told myself this incredible story, I visualised the day being filled with incredible people. I visualised what it would feel like to stand there, and I started to think about the energy that would be created between me and the audience – the power, the love, the vulnerability. And as I focused on that story, my nervous system began to respond to those emotions of love and connection. My system started to float in oxytocin, and as I exercised I started to produce endorphins, our endogenous morphine. I started to feel good; I started to feel calm. As we now know from research, as we exercise, our muscles release special chemicals called myokines, also known as 'hope molecules'. I was filled with hope.

I jumped off the treadmill, and started to shadowbox, punching all the way around the room, and as I punched, I breathed a lion's breath: *haa haa haa*. I could hear myself breathe, and I was regulating my vagus nerve. The vagus nerve plays such an important role in the mind–body connection. It is the longest of the cranial nerves, and it impacts all of our organs. The tone of the vagus nerve has a massive impact on how we think, how we feel and how we act. That simple act of chanting and breathing a lion's breath while I shadowboxed was strengthening the tone of my vagus nerve, and I was becoming alive.

I focused on my courage and my strength, and I said to myself again and again, 'Let's go, champ. Let's go, champ. Let's do this, champ.' I was now physically and chemically changing. I was firing neurons in my brain. I was attached to a vision that was no longer about the sleep I didn't get. I was attached to a vision of the incredible day I was about to have.

Forty-five minutes later, I felt like a new person. It didn't matter how much sleep I had or didn't have. What mattered now was who I was, what I believed and the day I wanted to manifest.

If the thoughts and emotions that flood our nervous system are not about hope and joy and love, that's perfectly okay. That is absolutely okay. But the choice we get every single morning when we wake is, is that my story? Are these the emotions I want to spend the rest of my day with, or is it time for a new story? **Every single morning, we wake up and we have a chance and a choice. A chance to start again, a chance to fall in love, a chance to be strong, a chance to be brave, a chance to go out and tell the world what we want.** And we get to choose to do that or not. Perhaps you choose to stay in bed, to engage in negative self-talk. Every single choice we make when we wake in the morning is either replaying that old negative self-defeating story or creating a new story that is uplifting, upregulating and inspiring. And the words we use have a massive impact on our choices.

As soon as you wake in the morning, listen to your inner story. And if it's not serving joy and love and peace, if it is not propelling you forward into a life of magnificence and a life where you step into your own power, then you get a chance to change it. And you can do that quite quickly from a multidimensional point of view: physically, chemically, biologically, energetically, spiritually. We can transform how we feel, how we think and how we act, and when we do that, we're going to transform the day ahead. And we can do that by scratching the record.

Scratch the record

If you're familiar with record players, you will know that, at times, the needle can get stuck, and when it does, it keeps playing the same line over and over.

If this isn't the piece of the song that we like most or if we are just tired of hearing this song, we know we must move the needle to change it. I use the idea of scratching the record to break free from a line we're stuck on with clients. It helps them to, firstly, become aware of the inner stories they are repeating and, secondly, to know they need to change these stories so they can hear a different song.

Many times throughout the day, when I find myself caught on a line, a word or a narrative that is not helping me, I have various techniques to move the needle or scratch the record. There are many ways in which we can interrupt our inner narrative and stop the repetition of a negative and unhelpful story. We can do this through, for example:

* Exercise

* Cold-water immersion

* Meditation

* Affirmations

* Journaling

* Visualisation

* Saying the story out loud so you are more likely to hear it for what it is

We need to be aware that when our inner story gets stuck on one line, we are the ones creating and perpetuating that story, and we at all times hold the power to move on to a different narrative.

We know from research and evidence that physical movement has a massive impact on our mental and emotional health. This happens for a number of different reasons.

First, we must remember that emotions are, in fact, a physical reality. The word 'emotion' comes from the French language and means 'physical disturbance'. Emotions create chemical and physiological realities that appear in the body as feelings. With every emotion comes a physical feeling, from metaphorical butterflies in our stomach to tears when we're sad or red cheeks when we're embarrassed, even having to go to the bathroom when we're nervous.

Movement, exercise and emotion

Each emotion we experience creates a physical change and manifestation in the body. So when we start to move the body, we can actually 'move' our emotions. Emotions are our energy in motion. There are no negative or positive emotions; they all contain important information. The only negative emotions are the ones we suppress and trap. So, when we start to move the body, we start to move that energy out of the body. That's why dancing is so fantastic for us. And yoga, Pilates or any exercise that moves the fascia – that connective tissue around every organ, blood vessel and bone in our body – release tension and stress.

When we exercise, the body also produces endorphins. Endorphins are endogenous morphine, which is an incredible chemical that allows us to feel elevated states of ease and bliss. When we exercise, when we dance, we are 'moving' our emotions and upgrading our chemistry.

When we move, we are building a sense of empower-ment, and *while* we move, if we are saying affirmations such as 'I am strong' and 'I am powerful' or if we are singing our favourite song, we are firing new neurons in the brain. We are literally creating new neurological pathways, and, as a result, we are priming the reticular activating system in the brain. We are telling ourselves that we want to see more joy, more love, more fun in the world. We want to see more opportunity. Exercise brings the brain, the nervous system, the reticular activating system and our chemistry in line. It releases stale-ness, stagnation and the old, while regenerating the new. One of the key ways to change our emotional state and our inner stories is to embrace the power of movement.

Exercise and our inner narrative

Exercise, or movement, has long been regarded as a staple in maintaining physical health, but its benefits extend far beyond just the physical realm. In recent years, numerous studies have shown the positive effects of exercise on our mental health, self-talk and self-confidence. Incorporating exercise into our daily routine can lead to improved overall well-being.

As well as benefiting our physical and mental health, exercise plays a key role in shaping our inner voice. Understanding the scientific benefits of exercise can help us to harness the power of physical activity to improve our inner narrative.

* **Mental health:** Physical activity triggers the release of endorphins, also known as 'feel-good' hormones, which can help alleviate symptoms of stress, anxiety and depression. Moreover, regular exercise has been shown to improve mood, cognition and memory, making it an effective tool for managing mental health conditions.

* **Self-talk:** Exercise can also influence our self-talk, or the internal dialogue we have with ourselves. Engaging in regular physical activity can boost feelings of self-worth, confidence and self-esteem. Additionally, achieving fitness goals through exercise can instil a sense of accomplishment and empowerment, leading to more positive self-talk and a healthier mindset.

* **Self-confidence:** Physical activity has been linked to enhanced self-confidence and self-efficacy. By pushing our physical limits and experiencing progress in our fitness journey, we can build resilience and confidence in our abilities. This new-found self-confidence can spill into other areas of our lives, empowering us to take on challenges and pursue our goals with determination and courage.

It is important to note that when we talk about exercise, we are not always talking about hard, intense, difficult exercise where we push ourselves to our limits. I do love intensive exercise, and I love difficult challenges, and at times it is exhilarating to really challenge ourselves and see where our limits lie – there's no doubt about that. However, when people are overly obsessed with this intensive, punishing exercise, I sometimes wonder if it is actually a positive thing. Or is it just another act of self-punishment and self-judgement?

I believe that exercise is like exorcism. An exorcism is to remove a ghost, and in this case the 'ghost' is negative energy. So exercise is as much about how it leaves you feeling emotionally as it has to do with the physical side of things. For me, the main thing is that exercise has to be varied. It should be joyous. It should make you smile and laugh. **Exercise is free play; it doesn't need a purpose, and it doesn't need to be timed or judged.** It can be any form of movement that shakes up and elevates our thoughts, our stories and our emotions. Exercise is what sets our souls free.

Here are some examples, based on research, of the significant impact movement can have on our lives:

* A study published in the *Journal of Psychiatric Research* found that individuals who engaged in regular physical activity had lower levels of anxiety and depression compared to sedentary individuals. Exercise was shown to be as effective as medication in reducing symptoms of depression in some cases.

* Research conducted at the University of Southern California revealed that regular exercise can modulate self-talk patterns and increase feelings of self-worth and self-efficacy. Participants who engaged in a consistent exercise regimen reported more positive self-talk and improved confidence in their abilities.

* Olympic athletes are prime examples of individuals who use exercise to cultivate self-confidence and positive

self-talk. By setting ambitious fitness goals, training diligently and pushing their physical boundaries, these athletes build resilience and self-assurance that enable them to perform at the highest level in their sport.

The scientific benefits of exercise on our mental health, self-talk and self-confidence are undeniable. By incorporating regular physical activity into our daily routine, we can reap the rewards of improved mood, reduced stress, enhanced self-talk and increased self-confidence. Harnessing the power of exercise can not only transform our physical health but also elevate our mental, emotional and psychological well-being. By prioritising fitness and self-care, we can pave the way for a healthier, happier and more confident life.

Visualisation

Visualisation is a simple but powerful technique whereby we create a strong mental image of a situation we want to prepare for or a skill we want to learn. Visualisation is a powerful tool because it fires and connects the brain's neurons and neural pathways in the same way that the actual physical experiences do. This means that we can build the necessary brain skills to perfect a skill, such as playing the piano, by visualising ourselves doing it. The more we see ourselves doing something perfectly in our minds, the more the brain believes we are doing it, so it becomes emotionally confident and assured about it. This means that when we have to execute the situation or skill in real life, not only do we have the necessary mental skills to execute it excellently, but we also now have the emotional skills to execute it with confidence and enthusiasm. This means we can increase motivation, enhance performance, improve focus and reduce stress by stimulating our brains through visualisation. By visualising success, you can build the self-confidence you need to succeed.

With all the clients I work with, especially the high-performance sports clients, I use visualising techniques to mentally rehearse for situations. By doing this, they are building a bank of powerful skills and emotions and, at the same time, eliminating any potential feelings of anxiety or nervousness.

The impact of this on our inner voice is immense. Because we have seen ourselves win over and over, and we have seen ourselves perform with confidence and ease, our brain and our nervous system are now creating a new narrative that says, 'I love being in these positions. I always deliver in these environments. I know I can execute this. I back myself.'

The challenge for most people is not just that they are not actively visualising the best possible outcome, but they are thinking about the worst possible outcome. Instead of seeing themselves succeed, they are seeing themselves fail. The more we see ourselves fail, the more our inner narrative becomes one of 'I can't do that, that's too scary for me, I wouldn't be able to handle that pressure.' Either way, the science is telling us that what we choose to visualise on a daily basis greatly impacts the story we tell ourselves. We get a choice: to keep visualising the worst possible outcome that creates a story of 'I can't', or to consciously start to visualise the best possible situation, what success looks like, what passion looks like, what fearlessness looks like, and create a new narrative of 'I can'.

How to visualise

Visualisation is a technique used to create mental images or scenarios in order to achieve a desired outcome or goal. It involves using your imagination to create a detailed picture of what you want to achieve, and then focusing on that image to increase motivation and manifest your goals.

Here is a simple guide to beginning your visualisation practice:

1. **Set your goal:** Start by identifying a specific goal or outcome that you want to achieve. This could be anything from improving your performance at work to increasing your confidence, or achieving a personal milestone.

2. **Create a mental image:** Find a quiet and comfortable space where you can relax without distractions. Close your eyes and start to visualise your goal as if it has already been achieved. Imagine the situation in as much detail as possible – what does it look like, sound like, feel like, smell like? Engage all of your senses to make the visualisation as vivid and real as possible.

3. **Embrace the emotions:** As you visualise your goal, focus on the emotions and feelings associated with achieving it. Feel the joy, excitement and sense of accomplishment as if it has already happened. This emotional engagement will help to reinforce the visualisation and make it more powerful.

4. **Stay focused:** Concentrate on your visualisation for a few minutes, allowing yourself to become fully immersed in

the experience. If your mind starts to wander, gently bring your focus back to the mental image of your goal.

5. **Repeat regularly:** Practise visualisation regularly to reinforce your goals and keep yourself motivated. You can do this daily or as often as you like, but consistency is key to making progress.

6. **Take action:** Visualisation is a powerful tool, but it works best when combined with action. Use the inspiration and motivation gained from your visualisations to take tangible steps towards your goals.

The power of affirmations

While most people may not be aware of it, we are at every moment practising and reinforcing affirmations. Every single word we say to others and to ourselves is being listened to and believed by our subconscious mind. As we have explored earlier, as these words are planted into our subconscious, our conscious brain will go into the world and select only the cues that match our internal beliefs and narratives. It is important that we become consciously aware of the things we are saying to ourselves, the things we say about ourselves and the things we say about the world. The words we use are the seeds from which our tomorrow grows.

Positive affirmations can have a significant impact on our brains and neurological connections and pathways. When we repeat positive affirmations, we are essentially rewiring our brains and reinforcing positive beliefs about ourselves. Here are some ways in which positive affirmations can influence our brains:

* **Neuroplasticity:** Our brains have the ability to change and adapt throughout our lives, a concept known as neuroplasticity. By consistently repeating positive affirmations, we can create new neural pathways and strengthen existing ones related to self-belief, self-worth and positivity (see p. 174 for more information on neuroplasticity).

* **Boosting self-esteem:** Positive affirmations can help to boost our self-esteem by reinforcing positive beliefs about ourselves. When we repeat affirmations that focus on our strengths and abilities, we are programming our brains to see ourselves in a more positive light.

* **Stress reduction:** Positive affirmations can help to reduce stress and anxiety by promoting a more positive and optimistic mindset. This can lead to the release of feel-good hormones like endorphins and dopamine, which can have a calming and mood-enhancing effect on the brain.

* **Improved cognitive performance:** Positive affirmations can enhance cognitive performance by fostering a more positive and confident mindset. When we believe in our abilities and potential, we are more likely to approach challenges with a growth mindset and perform at our best.

* **Emotional regulation:** Positive affirmations can help with emotional regulation by encouraging a more positive and balanced emotional state. By repeating affirmations that promote self-compassion and self-acceptance, we can cultivate a greater sense of emotional well-being.

Overall, positive affirmations can have a profound impact on our brain and neurological connections, promoting a more positive and resilient mindset. By incorporating positive affirmations into our daily routine and practising them consistently, we can rewire our brains for positivity and cultivate a more empowered and optimistic outlook on life.

Practising self-compassion through affirmations can help us to develop a kinder and more nurturing relationship with ourselves. Here are some affirmations to cultivate self-compassion:

* 'I am deserving of love and kindness, including from myself.'

* 'I acknowledge my mistakes and shortcomings with gentleness and understanding.'

* 'I release the need for perfection and embrace my perfectly imperfect self.'

* 'I grant myself permission to prioritise self-care and well-being.'

* 'I am worthy of forgiveness, both from others and from myself.'

* 'I choose to treat myself with the same compassion I offer to those I care about.'

* 'I embrace my humanness and allow myself to learn and grow from challenges.'

* 'I am enough just as I am, and I don't need to prove my worthiness to anyone.'

* 'I honour my needs and feelings, and I give myself the space to experience them without judgement.'

* 'I am strong, resilient and capable of overcoming obstacles with self-compassion as my guiding light.'

Repeat these affirmations regularly, especially during moments of self-doubt, criticism or adversity. They can help you to reframe negative self-talk, foster a sense of self-acceptance and cultivate a more compassionate inner dialogue. Remember that self-compassion is not a sign of weakness but a powerful tool for building resilience, self-esteem and emotional well-being.

CHAPTER 7
FINDING CALM IN THE
STORM: THE A-METHOD

Transform resistance into acceptance and acceptance into transformation

When we find ourselves caught in a negative spiral of thought – be that in a short-term situation where something in that moment is going against us and causing undue stress, fear, anxiety or anger, or in a longer-term situation – we find ourselves fixated and ruminating on it over the course of days, weeks or even months.

Whatever you are not actively changing, you are choosing. Whether it's that short-term moment or that longer-term situation, there comes a point at which we must make a decision about whether we are going to stay stuck in a spiral of negativity, anger, judgement and resistance or whether we are going to actively change our thoughts, stories and feelings.

We are never our situation, we are never the people around us, we are never what other people say about us, and we are never how people treat us. We must always remember that we are free and autonomous human beings, and while we don't always get to control what happens to us or how people treat us, we get to choose who we are and how we respond.

So, in every situation, there comes a moment of decision: to stay stuck or get unstuck. I use a process with my clients to first help them recognise when they have become stuck in a self-perpetuating negative cycle, and then help them get back to a state of calm, focus and aligned action.

This very simple process has four very simple steps:

1. Allow and accept
2. Acknowledge and reframe
3. Adjust
4. Align and act

1. Allow and accept

I can allow things and people to be as they are and say 'for the better'.

In the allow stage, we simply allow the situation to unfold. Just for a second, we allow the other person to think and act or behave as they are for that moment. We take our energy, awareness and attention from everything that is outside of our control, and we begin to place our energy, awareness and attention back onto ourselves for that split second or for that hour. We just allow things to be as they are.

For an athlete, this is allowing themselves to have made a mistake, to have dropped the point. The more we resist something and feel angry or fearful about it, the more we are trapped and controlled by that thing and that situation.

The moment we start to allow it is the moment we detach our energy, awareness and attention from the situation and bring it back to what we can control, which is ourselves. Then we accept – accept the situation for what it is, accept the mistake we have made, accept that somebody has treated us unfairly. This, of course, doesn't mean that we don't want to change the situation – we can absolutely want to change the situation. Acceptance means that we can then change it from a place of clarity and focus, not anger and chaos.

2. Acknowledge and reframe

Be the calm in the chaos.

The next step is to acknowledge that, in this moment or situation, you have a choice – to continue to be fixated on the negativity, judgement, resistance and chaos, or to become the calm in the chaos, to become the compassion in the anger, the light in the darkness. We have to accept that while we can't always control the external world, we are not defined by what happens to us but by how we choose to respond. We must always acknowledge that we have a choice in the nature, direction and tone of our inner thoughts and narratives.

In every situation, we must also acknowledge how our thoughts, emotions and actions are contributing to our unwanted situation. Under pressure, it is so easy to think all of the chaos is coming from and created by external people and sources, and this means that we often don't look inwards to see how we're the ones who are actually either creating or adding to the situation. I truly believe that, in most situations, we are at least 50 per cent of the chaos and we contribute at least 50 per cent to our own problems. And so, this simple but powerful acknowledgement gives us an immediate opportunity to reduce the stress, fear and anger in our own lives by at least 50 per cent.

3. Adjust

What would love do?

Step number three is to adjust – adjust your thinking and adjust the focus and direction of your thoughts and your inner narratives. A question I ask myself in these situations, which empowers me to adjust my thoughts from negative and resistant to positive and free, is: 'What would love do?' Similarly, if you know what your values are, if they are truth, honesty, love and compassion, then in that situation, ask yourself, 'What would kindness do?' Then adjust your thoughts, your feelings and your stories in line with those values.

When we adjust our thoughts, we either point them in the direction of fear or we point them in the direction of love.

4. Align and act

Now we align our actions with our intentions and our emotions. So if we have asked ourselves, 'What would love do?' or 'What would kindness do?', we immediately start to *act* from those places.

But how do we align our *intention* with our *attention*? By consistently affirming and visualising our desires through positive self-talk, we set clear intentions and signal to the universe what we want to manifest. This focused intentionality can help us attract opportunities, resources and people that support our goals and aspirations.

Intentional focus is where we actively guide our attention and awareness onto the very thing we want to experience more of and away from the thing we want to experience less of. Think of a golfer on a tee box. Imagine they are looking down the fairway and all they are thinking is, *Don't hit that bunker, don't hit that big bunker, don't hit that big bunker with all the sand in it.* The more they speak and focus their inner narrative on the bunker, the bigger the bunker gets in their mind and they are more likely to hit it. On the other hand, imagine the same golfer on the same tee box. They are fully aware of the bunker, but instead of running the narrative about how big and dangerous the bunker is, they are running a narrative about the incredible open space that is on the other side of the fairway. The more they focus their energy and attention on the open space, the more likely they are to hit their ball into that space.

Our human brain is not able to hear the word 'don't', so when we say, 'Don't think of a bunker', 'Don't think of a yellow elephant', 'Don't think of a red square', our brain immediately dismisses the word 'don't' and starts to think of the things we told it not to. If you don't want to focus on the bunker, think about the fairway; if you don't want to think about a red square, think about a blue circle.

And yet, partially because of our brain's strong negative bias, our inner voice spends more time speaking about what we don't want and where our pain is. The more we do this, the more we magnify and attract the things we don't want into our lives.

To manifest our intentions effectively, it is essential to cultivate a habit where we are consistently and actively running an inner story about the things we want, the things we love and the things we seek. By actively engaging in positive inner self-talk, by nurturing empowering beliefs and aligning our thoughts and emotions with the outcomes we desire, by practising mindfulness, gratitude and visualisation techniques, we can harness the power of our self-talk to manifest abundance, joy and success in our lives.

Once we have aligned our intention with our attention, the last step is to act. Go out and do it.

Yes, you can!

I know it is easy to read a chapter like this where someone like me is telling you about all the things that you CAN do and all the changes you CAN make and that you CAN live a life of abundance and joy and love. It is easy to read it, and it is easy to listen to somebody else saying it. But I know all too well that it's not always easy to believe it.

So why did I write this chapter? Why did I write this book with the passion and belief that, no matter who's reading it, it is absolutely possible that they can make incredible changes? You can release the past, you can change your stories, and you can manifest a life far more powerful than you can even imagine.

The reason I am so committed to this, the reason I believe in this so much, is that at one point in my life, I sat outside the office of my secondary school principal, in trouble again for being the class clown, which was my coping and deflection mechanism. I wasn't getting on well at school, and as I sat there, waiting to be disciplined again, on the outside I was acting tough. I was pretending I didn't care what was happening, that I didn't care about the teachers. That was my external presence, but my internal reality was that I did care. I cared that I was failing and that I was always in trouble. I did care about how I felt, which was scared and anxious and that I was a failure.

If somebody had told that boy sitting outside his principal's door, who believed his future was only filled with more fear, anger and failure, that he would grow up to be a global speaker and a best-selling author who would inspire, motivate and help millions of people all over the world, that he would go on to live a life of confidence and joy and love and courage, he might not have believed it either. But I believe it now. I know it's possible. I know the darkness the human soul can experience, I know hopelessness, I know loneliness, I know self-anger – but I also know that breaking free from all of those things is possible for every one of us.

This book, as with all of my books, is an expression of my life. With all my heart, I believe that no matter who you are, no matter what's happening in your life right now, no matter what has happened in your past, incredible change is possible for you, and a life of joy and love and ease and peace is our truest expression.

It is easy to read; it's not always easy to believe. But I'm here to give you hope and courage and confidence and the skills so that, no matter where you are right now, tomorrow can be whatever you want it to be, because you CAN write your own future.

CHAPTER 8
BELIEVE IN YOURSELF

Waking up the part of you that screams 'I CAN'

It is now time to turn the work back to you. I want to give you the framework to begin to identify the moments and opportunities where you have said 'I can'. As we work through previous situations where your inner voice was one of courage and strength, where you took assertive actions and stepped confidently in the direction of your dreams, let's remember what that felt like. Let's remember how powerful you felt in those moments. Let's remember what it was that gave you the courage and confidence to make those 'I can' statements and know that, even though you might have forgotten, you have that courage and strength within you. You have that incredible ability to say 'I can'.

In the second part of this section, we will start to look forward and, having awoken that inner strength and courage, that inner voice that says 'I can', we will identify the key areas in your life where 'I can't' becomes 'I can', 'I should' becomes 'I can' and 'I might' becomes 'I can'. We are going to look at the 'I can' statements that allow you, each and every morning, to make proactive decisions where you consciously direct your energy, awareness and attention towards what you *can* do and what you *do* have. By doing that, you take your energy, attention and awareness away from everything that you *don't* have.

By making these daily 'I can' statements, you are putting yourself in a mindset of empowerment. You are activating and awakening your inner coach. You are breaking your biggest challenges and tasks into small, achievable pieces. And instead of focusing on the whole thing, instead of focusing on the uncertainty and the adversity, you're going to focus your energy, awareness and attention onto what is achievable, what is controllable, what gives you a sense of courage and confidence. You're going to focus on what you *can* do.

Is your inner story magnifying the challenge or the solution?

We tend to overestimate the challenge and underestimate ourselves. If you are experiencing fear, self-doubt or uncertainty at this time, it can be overwhelming and scary. The more we focus our energy on the challenge, the bigger the challenge becomes; the less we focus our energy on ourselves, the more we shrink. With this, we are doing two things at the same time: we are magnifying the challenge and shrinking our ability to deal with it. On the other hand, if we focus on the moments we have shown courage, strength and ability, we magnify our power and minimise the challenge. The reason most people get stuck in a story of 'I can't' is because they magnify the challenge and minimise themselves. The mountain we face is simply the mountain – it doesn't change in size; but the way we think about it and the belief we hold in our own ability to climb that mountain is what makes it seem bigger or smaller.

In this first exercise, I will assist you in taking your focus, energy and attention away from whatever challenge you are facing and placing it back on you, your courage, your values and your successes. In doing so, I am going to help you remember that you are courageous, you are strong, you are adaptable, and you are more powerful than you even think.

List five moments in your life where you felt afraid but found the courage to do it anyway:

1. _____
2. _____
3. _____
4. _____
5. _____

List five times in your life where you doubted yourself, but you went on to prove your self-doubt wrong and achieved the thing you at one point doubted you could do:

1. _____
2. _____
3. _____
4. _____
5. _____

List five values you know you possess that make you proud:

1. _____
2. _____

3. _____

4. _____

5. _____

List five times you faced a situation you didn't expect and found the ability to adapt:

1. _____

2. _____

3. _____

4. _____

5. _____

Once we begin to remember that we *do* possess incredible capabilities and that we have shown these in the past, we can say, with a renewed energy and focus:

> **I am courageous.**
>
> **I am able to overcome self-doubt.**
>
> **I am committed to my values.**
>
> **I am adaptable.**

When you think about the challenge you are facing, think only about the things you can control.

List five things you can control:

1. _____

2. _____

3. _____

4. _____

5. _____

Instead of giving your energy to the things that might happen if it doesn't work out, identify five things that would happen if it does work out:

1. _____
2. _____
3. _____
4. _____
5. _____

List five things in your control that you can do every day to enable and empower you to be mentally and physically at your best:

1. _____
2. _____
3. _____
4. _____
5. _____

Empowered people have an empowered mindset that focuses on what they have, and not what they don't have. They have a mindset that is giving energy and attention not to the problem, but to the challenge. Empowered people don't overestimate the challenge ahead and neither do they underestimate themselves and their abilities. Empowered people begin with 'I can'; they begin with affirming thoughts that propel them into the right action with the right intention in the right direction.

Empowered people are not magical people; they are regular people who, at some point, got tired of playing small or apologising for their dreams. Empowered people realise life is short and that the quicker we let go of the past, other people's expectations and our self-limiting inner narratives, the quicker we get to start living life on our terms – a life of inner freedom, a life full of belief and ambition. The only question that remains is are you ready to become an empowered I CAN person? Because we can transform that 'I can' into 'I will' – and then everything begins to unfold.

TIME TO DO SOME WORK

Practical exercise: creating affirmations

We can all create affirmations that are specific and unique to our own circumstances and directly related to the outcomes and feelings we want to generate.

There are a few simple guidelines to creating powerful affirmations. The first one is the three P's:

1. Present tense
2. Personal
3. Positive

Affirmations are always written in the present tense – for example, 'I am happy today'. Our subconscious mind and our reticular activating system respond to affirmations better when things are happening now and not when we are thinking about something that will happen in the future. Similarly, our reticular activating system lights up brightest when we are speaking about ourselves, so keeping affirmations personal is key. Finally, we should use powerful words and statements about what we want and not use words or sentences about what we fear. This way we are giving our affirmations a positive direction.

The fourth important guideline is to experience the correct emotions as we repeat the affirmations. Affirmations are not just about words; they are equally about emotions. If your affirmation is about self-love, don't just say, 'I love myself'. Feel it. Imagine that warm, comforting feeling of self-acceptance washing over you. Embrace that self-love and let it radiate from within.

Create mantra affirmations

Think about the areas of your life that you'd like to change:

* Start with 'I' to shift your mindset – your thoughts need to be believable.

* Keep it present tense.

* Use a motivating adjective or verb.

* Be positive, focused.

* Be concise.

* Begin with the end in mind.

* Start with 'I am' and 'I have'.

* Be specific.

* Say it with feeling.

* Consistency is key: use them every day.

Sample affirmations for self-confidence

* I radiate self-confidence and inner strength.

* I am unstoppable and resilient in the face of challenges.

* I trust my intuition and follow my heart with confidence.

* I am the architect of my own destiny, and I am creating a life I love.

* I am a powerful force for good in the world, and I make a positive impact wherever I go.

* I am deserving of all the good things that come into my life.

* I am a valuable and important person who contributes positively to the world.

* I am bold, courageous and confident in all that I do.

* I am a magnet for success, abundance and happiness.

* I am confident, capable and worthy of all the blessings life has to offer.

Awakening inner freedom and abundance affirmation

An audio recording of this affirmation can be accessed on my website https://www.gerryhussey.ie/i-am-i-can-i-will-meditations with the password IAMICANIWILL.

I am ready.

I am more than ready.

I am perfectly ready to change.

To allow and facilitate this change, I am making commitments and promises to myself. These commitments and promises I will honour and uphold each and every day.

I am now ready to allow myself to change, allow myself to become a person of truth, love and clarity.

I am committing with all my heart to stop playing small.

I am committing to stop downplaying my own value and worth.

I am committing to stop worrying about what other people think of me and other people's opinions.

I am born to stand out.

So I am now committing to stop trying to fit in.

I am allowing myself to be me.

I am allowing myself to release my pain. I am allowing myself to release my past.

I am allowing myself to release and let go of everything that no longer serves me.

I am stepping out of my past.

I am cutting the emotional cords and connection that have been tying me to my past.

I understand that this was part of my story.

This was part of my identity.

But it no longer is.

I no longer need to hold on to my past.

I commit to stepping firmly and confidently into my future; the great unknown is a great opportunity where I get to write a new story.

I AM. I CAN. I WILL.

I am committing to this new story being one of my own making.

One that is driven by my dreams, not my fears.

One that is driven by love and not fear.

I am allowing myself to renew; I am allowing every cell and sinew in my body to renew.

I am allowing love to find me easily.

I am allowing forgiveness to flood to my heart and my soul.

I am allowing abundance to find me easily.

I am committing to an abundant mindset where I focus on what I have, no longer on what I don't have.

I am committing to gratitude.

I am committing to living in a more grateful state of being.

I am allowing myself to make mistakes, and when I do, I will quickly recognise the mistake and move on.

I am allowing myself to try new things.

I am allowing myself to be new.

I am an incredible human being.

I have an incredible soul.

I am enough, I have always been enough, and I will always be enough.

I place my hand on my heart, firmly in the hand and heart of the Divine.

I release myself from the human ego.

I step firmly with faith and confidence into this great expansive universe.

My words become the seeds from which tomorrow grows.

I am committing to using words of kindness and love, words that inspire and uplift both me and the people I come in contact with.

I am committing to being a beacon of truth and authenticity, where I speak freely and openly with respect and with love.

I am allowing myself to surround myself with people who uplift and inspire me.

I am allowing myself to release myself from people who no longer inspire or uplift me.

I am releasing myself from people who make me feel not enough.

In this one short, beautiful life, I will now take every opportunity and I will see each and every morning as a chance to begin again.

I now recognise that each and every morning I have a chance.

A chance to begin again.

A chance to fall in love.

A chance to see the sunrise.

A chance to inspire.

A chance to uplift.

A chance to show the world who I am.

And I have a choice.

A choice whether to do something or not.

From now on I am committing to no longer be defined by what happens in my life.

I will no longer be defined by things I can't control.

I will place my energy, awareness and attention firmly into the things that I can control.

I will be defined not by what happens to me, but by how I choose to respond.

I am a powerful, conscious creator of my own life.

I am no longer a passive participant.

Life is no longer happening to me, it is happening for me, and I am ready to step into my own power.

There is nothing enlightened about shrinking so that others won't feel insecure around me.

I am committing to no longer shrinking.

I step into my power. I step into my magnificence. I step into my dreams with ease and joy and love and grace.

Meditation

A meditation to cultivate self-empowerment

An audio recording in which I guide you through this meditation can be accessed on my website https://www.gerry hussey.ie/i-am-i-can-i-will-meditations with the password IAMICANIWILL.

To begin a meditation practice focused on self-empowerment, find a quiet and comfortable space where you won't be disturbed. Settle into a relaxed but alert posture, either seated or lying down. Close your eyes and take a few deep breaths to centre yourself.

* Connect with your breath. Start by bringing your awareness to your breath. Notice the sensation of air entering and leaving your body. Allow your breath to slow down and deepen, bringing a sense of calm and presence.

* Imagine roots growing from the soles of your feet, anchoring you deep into the earth. Feel the support and stability of the earth beneath you, grounding you.

* Repeat empowering affirmations in your mind such as 'I am strong, capable and worthy', 'I trust in my abilities and intuition', or 'I am deserving of happiness and success'. Repeat these affirmations with conviction and belief in their truth.

* Visualise your empowered self. Envision yourself as confident, resilient and empowered. See yourself achieving your goals, overcoming challenges and embracing your true potential. Visualise a bright and radiant light shining from within you, illuminating your path forward.

* Embrace self-love. Practice self-compassion and self-love by showering yourself with kindness and acceptance. Acknowledge your inherent value as a unique and worthy individual.

* Generate gratitude. Reflect on the blessings and positive aspects of your life. Feel gratitude for the strength and resilience that have brought you to this moment and for the opportunities that lie ahead.

* Slowly bring your awareness back to the present moment. Take a few deep breaths, gently wiggle your fingers and toes, and open your eyes. Carry the sense of empowerment and self-love with you as you go about your day.

I AM. I CAN. I WILL.

Repeat this meditation regularly to cultivate a sense of empowerment, resilience and self-love in your life. Trust in your inner strength and capabilities, and remember that you have the power to create the life you desire.

Summary of Section 2: I Can

*   Beware the power of the tribe and groupthink.

*   Shitty people with shitty beliefs tell themselves and others shitty stories to justify their shitty decisions and shitty actions.

*   Scratch the record by exercising, visualising and telling yourself that you're good enough – because you are!

*   Remember times that you have drawn on your courage and power. Reawaken that self-belief.

SECTION 1:

I AM

SECTION 2:

I CAN

SECTION 3:

I WILL

CHAPTER 9
BREAK THE RECORD

Take the story and reframe it

In section one, we focused on 'I am' and we looked at how we became the people we are right now, how we have created our inner stories, our deepest beliefs and our self-fulfilling inner narratives.

I highlighted that no matter where you are right now, no matter what your inner story is right now, no matter what the tone and nature of your self-talk is right now, you are always capable of change.

I am not my past.

I am not my environment.

I am not what other people want me to be.

I am not here to shrink and play small.

I am more powerful than I can imagine.

I am free to let my past go.

I am free to step into a new future.

I am free to live a life on my terms.

When we start to make more powerful 'I am' statements and we redefine what we truly are, we begin to get ready for change ...

In section two, we entered the 'I can' phase. This phase ignited an inner belief that change is possible, but also the knowledge that *you* are the one who can change. The 'I can' phase was about self-empowerment and a deep commitment to stop waiting around for someone else to come and save you or give you permission to change. We looked at taking back your inner power, your autonomy and your sense of control, and instead of giving your energy, attention and awareness to what you *can't* do, you are, from now on, going to focus on what you *can* do.

In this section, we will now focus on 'I will.' I will go through some simple, powerful and practical ways that every one of us can commit to in order to actively change, disrupt and build a whole new narrative that propels us into a new life of greater ease, joy, love and freedom.

Our lives are not changed by what we know – our lives are changed by what we do. So, in this section, we will build 'I will' statements that will enable you to get to a position where:

You WILL set yourself free.

You WILL release your past.

You WILL build a new, more powerful story.

You WILL quieten your inner critic and awaken your inner coach.

The first step is saying I am capable of change, the second step is awakening that inner belief that I can, and the final step is a powerful commitment to I will.

Let's begin.

Let go of the entrapment narrative

I was at a retreat once with my wife, which was facilitated by the amazing life coach Ian Kingston. He was running a session during which he was trying to get us to a whole new level of awareness about who we are and how we have come to be that person. A key part of understanding how we have become who we are is exploring the inner and outer stories we tell and buy into, how these stories feed into our deepest subconscious beliefs, and how these stories, at times, become our entrapment narrative. The more we repeat and buy into these stories, the more our life becomes a repeating cycle of fulfilling these stories.

At an important part of the facilitation, Ian was holding a coaching conversation with my wife, Miriam. He was asking her to think of the characteristics she holds that make her special and powerful, and also the characteristics that are holding her back – the ones she would like to change.

One of the things Miriam spoke about wanting to change was her need to be a people-pleaser and how people-pleasing and solving problems for other people was something that was deep in the heart of who she was.

When the facilitator explored this in greater detail, he asked her if these characteristics were something she was born with or something she developed. Miriam was aware that she had created some of these characteristics and that she wasn't necessarily born with them, but as she talked, she repeated something very simple but something that was really important. She spoke about the different roles she played in her family: about being the problem-solver and the peacemaker, and the expectations and pros and cons of being the youngest in the family. The phrase 'the youngest in my family' came up a number of times while she spoke.

When she was finished, the facilitator took a moment and allowed the room to be silent, and then he said something truly powerful, something that if my wife wasn't open to it, or if she wasn't really up for change, she could have easily taken offence to. He asked Miriam, 'When are you going to stop telling yourself that shitty story?'

In one way, the story of her being the youngest is a simple fact, but what the facilitator was getting at was far deeper. It wasn't the fact that she was the youngest: it was the fact that she had inherited or created beliefs about how the youngest should behave and how they should engage with their family. She had created an inner story about being the youngest that in many ways justified or explained her own state of being. Rightly or wrongly, she accredited her characteristics to being the youngest. By the facilitator asking her, 'When are you going to let go of that shitty story?', he was reminding her that being the youngest is not a reason to be or not be a certain way. He was reminding her that she was a powerful and autonomous human being with incredible potential regardless of where she came in the family. He was saying that her story had to change from being 'the youngest' to being 'powerful and dynamic and inspirational'.

We often tell ourselves stories to justify our habits and patterns. That story might be *I am this way because of my past/where I'm from/the school I went to/the family I grew up in/the boss I have/the place I work*. At times, the way we are choosing to be is less than our true potential, and as long as we tell ourselves that story, that's just the way it is. We are giving the story our power by saying, 'That's just the way I am.'

Tell me that story again, but tell it differently

Anybody who's read my other books will know how important a gentleman called Ravi is in my life. He is my coach, my mentor and my friend, and he has an amazing mind, with an incredible ability to explain the human ego and the ways it can keep us trapped and struggling if we don't elevate our consciousness to our higher self, the observer self. I could not have got through the last few years without him.

He has helped me to achieve a new level of understanding and awareness about myself. When I was stuck in my own negative stories and negative emotions, he carefully and lovingly challenged me through his somatic coaching and his understanding of how the human ego can create so much of our inner struggles and experiences of life. Ravi is a coach to whom I owe many of my greatest breakthroughs.

On one occasion, I had returned from Portugal to Ireland to do some work with a corporate organisation. After the event, there was a mix-up with my travel and I ended up missing my flight. I had an important event with an important client in Portugal the following day, and this meant I would have to reschedule or cancel it. I rang Ravi to see if he happened to have an appointment available; if I was going to spend an extra evening in Dublin, I thought it would be useful to try to connect with him. Luckily, Ravi had a space available, and a few hours later I found myself telling him all about my stressful day – missing my flight, trying to rearrange the schedule and worrying that my client in Portugal might not be understanding because it was going to negatively impact them.

Ravi, as he does, listened carefully, and after I had finished telling him my story of woe and stress, he replayed my story through the lens of a different emotion, from a different perspective. Ravi said, 'If you will allow me, let me tell you that story again. You have a house in Dublin yet you get to spend many months every year in Portugal. You have incredible clients in Ireland and incredible clients in Portugal. You get to travel back and forth between Ireland and Portugal regularly to spend time with these amazing clients, and by doing work that you truly love and that inspires you, you get to meet incredible people and have incredible experiences. And on this one trip, while getting to work, a flight has been missed which now gives you the opportunity to stop, rest and reset. And by opening your mind and your heart to new possibilities, this will lead to a greater place.'

Ravi looked at me and said, 'The main point of that story is you have a successful business, you work at something you love, you are lucky enough to work with amazing clients who you deeply care about. What part of that story is causing you stress?'

It was a shock – it was the kick in the backside that I needed. Ravi looked me straight in the eye and said, 'My dear, now tell me that story again, but tell it in a different way.' **It is often not the situation that causes our stress or anger or suffering: it is the tone in which we tell it – the part of the situation, the moments and characters we choose to focus on.** We need to tell ourselves the same story again, but tell it in a different way.

So now is the time to start telling yourself *your* story in a different way. There are several techniques that can help enhance our self-talk and cultivate a more positive and empowering inner dialogue.

* **Practise self-awareness:** Pay attention to your inner monologue and identify any negative or self-critical thoughts. Awareness is the first step towards changing your self-talk.

* **Challenge negative thoughts:** When you notice negative self-talk, challenge those thoughts with evidence or alternative perspectives. Ask yourself if those thoughts are based on facts or assumptions.

* **Practise self-compassion:** Treat yourself with kindness and empathy, just as you would a friend. Be understanding and forgiving of your mistakes and shortcomings.

* **Use positive affirmations:** Create and repeat positive affirmations to counteract negative self-talk. Affirmations are simple statements that reflect the qualities you want to embody, such as 'I am confident and capable.'

* **Surround yourself with positivity:** Surround yourself with supportive and uplifting people who encourage positive self-talk. Avoid environments or individuals that feed into negative self-talk.

* **Engage in activities that boost self-esteem:** Engage in activities that make you feel good about yourself, such as exercising, pursuing hobbies or volunteering. The more you engage in activities that boost your self-esteem, the more positive your self-talk will become.

* **Seek professional help if needed:** If negative self-talk is persistent and impacting your mental well-being, consider seeking help from a therapist or counsellor. They can provide strategies and support to help you enhance your self-talk and improve your mental health.

By practising these strategies consistently, you can gradually shift your inner dialogue in a more positive and constructive direction, leading to increased self-confidence, resilience and well-being.

Would you be willing to allow me to give you a different perspective?

There is a beautiful expression that I use in working with clients when I become aware that there is a story that they are buying into and allowing to dominate their actions and decisions – a story that is keeping them trapped in their current state of unhappiness.

It is not always easy to tell somebody that the story they are telling is wrong. It is not my job to pick holes in their story, and sometimes if we challenge that deeply held story, people become defensive and argumentative, so our ability to help them will be lost. In a situation where I'm working with somebody with a deeply held belief that is no longer helping them or enabling them, I will listen intently, making sure they know they are being listened to, and only after they have finished telling their story will I ask them, 'Would you be willing to allow me to give you a different perspective?'

Very often the angle from which we look at something impacts how we interpret it. When we have an internal emotion, an internal expectation or pressure, the external situation becomes tainted or manipulated by it. When we allow somebody who is objective – somebody who can see the same situation without our subjective pressures and expectations – to look, they see it through a different lens and without the unhelpful emotional attachments.

We must be willing to allow other people to give us a different perspective. My question is beautiful but simple – it is not confrontational and it does not dismiss the story you are telling. It is a loving question, an empowering question, a clear question. Would you be willing to allow me to give you a different perspective?

Meeting our uncomfortable truth

There is a concept I use with my clients called meeting our uncomfortable truth. As mentioned earlier when we spoke about the human ego, our ego is always trying to protect us from pain and extinction. To do this, it will employ many different techniques and can be relentless in its mission to protect us, or at least in doing things that it *thinks* protects us.

One of the things the ego fears most is looking at its own role in our suffering and looking at where we, our actions, our emotions and our stories might actually be untrue.

Meeting an uncomfortable truth is where we dare to move outside the need to serve the ego and instead open our minds and hearts to what actually might be the real truth. First, we must be willing to put ourselves in the way of people, information and situations that challenge our ego-based thinking, and second, we must then be willing to allow this new information or challenge to be absorbed and processed without resistance. Once we allow our own position to be assessed by ourselves without judgement, we can often begin to encounter an uncomfortable truth.

To show just how attached to our inner beliefs and stories we can be, I will tell a famous story about a man who goes to a psychiatrist because the man believes he is a statue.

After chatting together for quite a while, the man tells the psychiatrist over and over again that he is a statue and that he has been a statue for the last couple of months. The psychiatrist listens carefully and slowly tries to bring the man to a new level of awareness where he begins to realise that he is, in fact, a human being and not a statue. But the man is attached to the belief that he is a statue, so the psychiatrist uses different questions and different scenarios to bring that man to awareness.

Eventually he asks the man, 'Do statues bleed?' The man says, 'Of course statues don't bleed.' 'Okay,' says the psychiatrist. He stands up and asks the man, 'May I have your arm for a moment?' The man obliges, and the psychiatrist takes a small needle and pricks the man's skin. A small bit of blood appears. Confused, the man looks at the blood coming out of his arm. He seems puzzled.

The psychiatrist says, 'What do you see?' The man replies, 'I see that I'm bleeding.' The psychiatrist asks, 'Does that change anything?' 'Yes,' the man replies, 'that changes everything – it changes my whole belief.'

'What's your new belief?' asks the psychiatrist.

'Well, it's obvious,' the man says. 'Statues *do* bleed.'

The man was unwilling to let go of the idea that he was a statue. The only story that he was willing to change was a story about statues. When we cling to a deeply held belief or story, our ego will manipulate every other aspect of the situation. It will create multiple new and varying stories, but it will not at any point be willing to give up the original story, whether that is true or not.

As we begin to change our deepest beliefs, it can be uncomfortable and we may experience fear and feelings of anxiety as our ego attempts to prevent us from changing. Just like an airplane must experience turbulence as it elevates to a higher altitude, we often experience emotional turbulence as we start to elevate our awareness and understanding. But just as the airplane needs to move through the turbulence to get to the level it needs to be at, we must be willing to allow ourselves to move through the uncomfortable truths to get to the level we need to be at.

So become a little more aware of when you might be meeting your uncomfortable truth. Listen to your inner stories and ask if they have been constructed to avoid an uncomfortable truth. Ask yourself, 'Why am I really finding it hard to hear this other story?'

We need to realise there is often an incredible awakening and growth opportunity when we become comfortable with being open to our uncomfortable truths.

What are you prioritising by telling that story in that way?

When we become aware of how we respond in certain situations, we might notice that we use 'shrinking words', language whereby we retreat from our true power. It is important to ask in those moments, what are we actually prioritising when we prioritise social acceptance over self-expression? When we are so afraid of upsetting people in case they abandon us or in case the tribe leaves us behind, it means we will always communicate in a way that first and foremost gets us accepted.

In every conversation that we have, both inwardly and outwardly, we are prioritising something: maybe it's the ego, the need to fit in, the need to be seen and heard in a certain way, the need to fit into other people's beliefs about us. **When we begin to prioritise self-expression and self-identity, we can begin to speak with truth and honesty.** When we begin to prioritise our dreams, our ambitions, our deepest inner wisdom and the expressions of our powerful soul, we become truthful, authentic and powerful communicators. As you hear yourself communicate in any situation, ask yourself, 'By speaking like this, by using these words and by using this tone, what am I prioritising?'

CHAPTER 10
THE TOOLS OF
TRANSFORMATION

Tell yourself a different ending

The ability to reframe any story at any moment is essential to make sure that the thoughts and stories we are feeding our brain and our nervous system are ones that bring clarity, focus and the right energy. Our stories can be reframed into ones that give us a sense of control, autonomy and freedom.

There will always be parts of a story that might be messy and not as we would choose. Parts of our story might even bring us pain. But in every story, in every situation, no matter how small, there is a glimmer of light. There is something that is joyful and special and precious, and no matter how difficult the situation is, we can seek, hope and strive for a different outcome.

In those difficult moments, why not tell an incredible story about the future? If the current situation is one of hopelessness, why not inspire yourself with an amazing story about how it's all going to unfold? Tell yourself a story about the magnificent ending that's going to follow.

When we reframe our stories, we are saying, 'I am taking my energy, awareness, attention and power away from what I don't want', and when it is all over, the most important story will not be about the situation, but instead about how we responded to it. No matter what you're facing, reframe it to create a powerful vision of the future, one that uplifts, and go after that.

The day I learned how a truly great coach speaks

Ding, ding!

I'm sitting ringside and the fighter I am there to support has just finished the eleventh round of his world-title fight. The arena is packed with his supporters, his closest friends and his family, who have travelled across the world to be there to see him perform and witness his magnificence. The moment I look up at the people there to support him, I can immediately tell by their faces and their body language that they are feeling the same way I am: anxious, surprised, deflated.

I turn my gaze back to the ring to see the fighter as he walks to the corner for the last time. So much expectation, years of dreaming and sacrificing, a lifetime of setbacks and comebacks all culminating in this one moment. Yet round by round, not only has the fight slipped away from him, but also, for a reason we can't understand, a spark, an energy has been missing. As a consequence, his opponent has jumped on the opportunity to steal away everything he has dreamed of.

160

As the fighter reaches the corner and takes a seat, I can see his face is marked and bruised, and blood is running freely from a big cut above his eye. But these aren't the things that stand out to me. It's like his soul has been bleeding from the very start of the fight, and as he sits in the corner for the last time, it is like hope has evaporated and all that is left is fatigue and sadness.

He sits on the stool, looking at the ground, his shoulders slumped. As an ex-boxer who has lost more fights than I care to remember, I know what he is thinking: 'How can this be happening? Why me? Why now?' He is already thinking about how he is going to explain this underperformance to people; he is thinking about all the money people spent coming to see him; he is thinking of all the people he is letting down. Deep in his heart, he is probably hoping a hole will open up and swallow him rather than having to deal with the embarrassment and regret.

Twelve rounds in a professional fight is a long, long time. It's 36 of the toughest minutes imaginable, and when you are exhausted and your opponent is coming with everything they have, a minute can seem like a lifetime – so 36 minutes can feel like an eternity.

Because I am sitting ringside, I can hear the conversation that's unfolding between the coach and the fighter, and over the next 35 seconds I witness one of the greatest coaching moments I have ever seen.

As the boxer walked back lifeless, his eyes staring at the ground, the coach jumped into the ring as if the fighter had won the last 11 rounds. Everything in the coach's energy was radiating calmness, passion, joy and belief. The coach stood right in front of the boxer, placed his hand on the boxer's

161

heart and told him to look up. 'Look into my eyes,' the coach screamed with excitement. 'Get that chin up, champ – look at me.' When the boxer eventually raised his head, the coach, with a smile on his face, said, 'Breathe, just breathe,' and the boxer began to take some deep breaths. The coach, still calm and relaxed, took deep breaths with the boxer and created a connection between them. There was an unspoken magic; something was happening.

With his hand still firmly on the boxer's heart, the coach's smile grew. The two men were in unity, so the coach had the opportunity to speak not just to the boxer's mind, but to his heart and his soul.

The coach said, 'Now listen to me, listen only to me – you might have a story beginning to build in your head, and that story might be that you've lost all eleven rounds and that your jab isn't working and that your feet feel flat and that you've let everybody down and you can't believe what's happening. Now let me tell you another story ...' The expression on the coach's face went from happy and excited to focused and assured, and he continued: 'I want you to really listen to this story – I want you to listen to it with all your heart. The other story is that I believe in you, I trust you, and I love you. No matter what happens in the next three minutes, I will love you and I will be so proud of you. I will be proud of who you are and everything you have done for me and every experience you have allowed me to have, memories I will treasure forever. It doesn't matter to me what happens here; it doesn't matter to the people who love you – they will always love you because they love you. It's not about us: it's about you, and I am asking you to listen to me.

'We might never get this opportunity again, so I want you to look around. I want you to see the arena, I want you to see all the people who love you and believe in you, I want you to see their eyes, because they still believe in you, and they still know that this is possible.

'Now I'm going to give you a new story: you have knocked out loads of people in the past. I have seen you knock out multiple people in your career. I've seen you knock out multiple people in training camps. I know you can knock out people and I know to knock out someone you only need a split second. You have three more minutes to find that split second, and if you can find it, you're going to knock this guy out and you're going to become a champion.'

When I looked at the boxer, it was like a different fighter was standing there: his tired shoulders were upright and alert; it was as if his eyes were looking into the coach's soul – a spark had appeared. There was a whole new mission and a whole new energy.

The coach moved his hand from the boxer's heart and placed it on the side of his face. 'Come on, champ,' he said. **'I need you to listen to this story, I need you to believe in this story, because I believe it with all my heart. I believe in it with all my soul, and I have never been more certain of anything in my life.'**

The conversation took no more than 35 seconds, yet it had connected with something deep in the heart of the boxer. It had reignited his hope, passion, focus, ambition and determination. It had rewritten his story.

When the boxer walked to the centre of the ring, there was a smile on his face and certainty in his eyes. For the first time in the fight, his opponent looked unnerved. The final round started, and for the next two minutes and forty-two seconds it was a war. For those two minutes and forty-two seconds, the boxer looked for an opening, looked for that split-second opportunity, and when it appeared, he took it. With 18 seconds left on the clock, his opponent hit the canvas and was counted out. With 18 seconds left on the clock, the tide had changed and what seemed like a hopeless situation had just become the greatest moment of his life.

Simple changes to activate empowerment

We know from the incredible work of neuroscience that our nervous system works hand in hand with our inner thoughts and stories, activating chemical and physiological responses in our body as they respond to every word we say, both to ourselves and to other people. These chemical and physiological changes in our body mobilise a million different responses in our system, and the culmination of those responses either puts us in a place of empowerment, where we act with clarity, or puts us in a place of disempowerment, where we're uncertain and we retreat.

We've all heard of the fight, flight, freeze and flow responses our bodies can have. Each of these reactions will have its own impact on how you think, feel and act.

If we're in a particular situation and use words that are threat based, the brain activates the amygdala, which is part of the limbic system, our stress centre, and it shuts down our prefrontal cortex, which is the part of the brain responsible for reasoning, logic and creativity.

Our brain then starts to produce chemicals such as cortisol and adrenaline, which in the short term have a positive impact. Short-term use of our fight or flight response allows us to develop resilience and new emotional capabilities. But over the long-term, the chemicals produced by the brain in this fight or flight mode impair our decision-making and reasoning skills. This robs us of our ability to be present in the moment. Being in stress mode is not always the enemy; staying in prolonged stress mode is the real enemy.

On the other hand, when we use words and sentences that are opportunity based, even though we might still be in the same situation, our brain does not produce the same levels of cortisol and adrenaline. In fact, it produces chemicals such as oxytocin, which is an incredible hormone that makes us feel safe and loved.

Here are some examples of how we can reframe the sentences and words that are threat based into ones that are opportunity based so we get that all-important oxytocin into our systems during times of challenge.

Threat-driven phrases	Opportunity-driven phrases
It's hard	It's an exciting challenge
But	And
I need to	I will
I have to	I get to
It's not easy	It's challenging me to be stronger
It's hard to make money	With the right plan money finds me easily
It's hard to meet someone romantically	I know the right person is waiting for me

| I am not very confident | I am committing to becoming a confident person |
| I hate public speaking | I embrace the challenge of becoming a great public speaker |

Words as nutrition

Just as there are differences in food, there are differences in words.

There are foods that have a high nutritional value, and there are foods that have a low nutritional value. When we eat foods of high nutritional value, we don't need a lot of that food. Each piece of food with a high nutritional value serves a purpose. It sustains energy, it helps balance our nervous system, it hydrates our body, it lowers inflammation. When we eat foods of high nutritional value, we eat less and have fewer issues with weight, fewer issues with managing our appetite, fewer issues with cravings and fewer health issues.

On the other hand, when we eat food with low nutritional value, we are always hungry, because our body is simply not being nourished and is not getting the vitamins or minerals it needs to live a life of vitality, health and wellness. When we eat food of low nutritional quality, we need more of that food, yet no matter how much more we eat, it is still unable to nourish us. We consume a lot of it, but it never seems to give us what we need. In fact, it often gives us what we don't need or want.

Processed food can have a massive negative impact not just on our gut health, but also on our mental health. It can deplete our mind as well as our body.

With so much information about food quality, food production and nutritional value, awareness of its effects is very much in the mainstream, and people are looking for food of high nutritional value.

But just as food nourishes the body, it is also important to see our language and the way we communicate as a form of food that nourishes our soul, our mind and our nervous system. Just as we can have food with a high or a low nutritional value, we can have language that is of high or low nutritional value.

When we use words that inspire and empower us, we don't need big long statements. We don't need to be speaking all the time. One word, one statement can be powerful enough.

On the other hand, when we use words that have no nutritional value, we might find ourselves speaking all the time, but it has little effect, or at least little positive effect. It can, however, have a massive negative effect. When we find our thoughts going around in circles, yet we don't seem to be able to find strength and courage, it's because our soul is not getting what it needs from our communication style to be vibrant, healthy and impactful.

And just as processed food can have a negative impact on our body, certain words can have a negative impact on our soul and on our nervous system – words such as 'should' and 'but'. I'll explore some of these words below, but first let's look at a new type of food pyramid – one that shows us the value certain words and phrases have. Using this 'inner voice pyramid', you can make sure the language calories you're taking in are giving you energy, not taking it. At the top of the pyramid are words we tend to use from time to time, but we can try to use less of. You can become more conscious of these words by keeping track of how many times you say 'but' or 'I can't' or 'I have to' today.

You can then swap these words for ones that provide your mind and body with more sustenance, which you'll find in the middle row. These words are useful for reframing your inner dialogue when you catch yourself engaging in unhelpful self-talk – 'and', 'yes', 'I get to'.

In the bottom row of the pyramid you will find phrases that I would like you to say to yourself at every opportunity. Think of them as if they are your 'five-a-day' – phrases full of goodness that will boost your mood. Just as we can forget to eat well during stressful periods, we can also lose sight of how amazing we are when we're at a low ebb, so these simple phrases really pack a punch. Eat as much as you like.

This simple word food pyramid gives us a visual reminder that the words we're using are either nourishing us and making us healthy and stronger or depleting our energy and robbing us of vitality and strength. I would love if you began to use this pyramid as a simple challenge to yourself to see how many of the life-giving words and expressions you can use throughout the day and to be more aware about avoiding words that deplete your energy, your vitality and your health.

Once we have this new awareness, we can use this pyramid to challenge ourselves, to reshape the type of language we are consuming, whether we're speaking to other people or to ourselves. We are consuming the nature and the tone of everything we say, and that is having an impact on our health and well-being.

At the end of each day, sit down and ask yourself, *How many of those self-empowering words and expressions did I use today?* Try to remember the moments and situations in which you used them. And if, for some reason, you don't succeed on some days, please do not bring judgement or criticism into it. This exercise is not about punishing ourselves. When we have a day where our word nutrition hasn't been good, we accept it, acknowledge it and then release it. But think back to the situations where perhaps you could have used slightly better or more empowering words. Identify the moments in which there was an opportunity for change and commit to being a little more consciously aware of your words. It could be simple moments, such as when you're buying something in a shop and somebody asks, 'How are you?' Instead of saying, 'I'm fine' or 'I'm okay', maybe say, 'I'm magnificent'. If a friend or colleague starts to talk about the past or the future, remind them of something extraordinary that's happening in this moment.

This pyramid gives us a simple scoring system to help us be mindful of the words we're using in everyday situations, and to make sure those words are uplifting, inspiring and making us healthier and stronger.

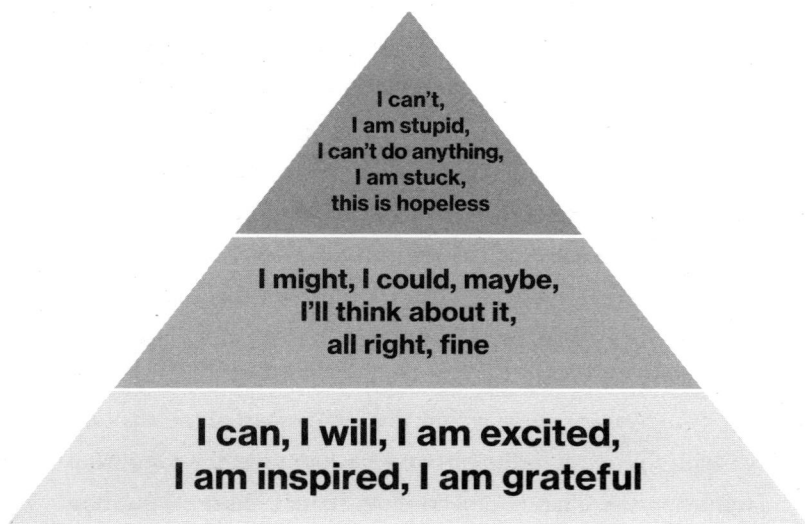

I can't,
I am stupid,
I can't do anything,
I am stuck,
this is hopeless

I might, I could, maybe,
I'll think about it,
all right, fine

**I can, I will, I am excited,
I am inspired, I am grateful**

Sometimes we need to change the entire story – sometimes we simply need to change one word

The whistle goes, the stadium erupts. A player I have been working with has scored one of the most magnificent goals ever seen in Croke Park, the home of Gaelic games in Ireland. It is a mecca for GAA fans. The stadium is steeped in history and legends, hallowed turf where dreams are made reality for the victors. This moment, this comeback by the team I am working with, will go down as one of the greatest comebacks of all time.

The noise is deafening. The release of emotion is phenomenal. It is an explosion of generations of hope, dedication, belief and sacrifice. And now joy and love and gratitude are pouring from every single player and coach, and every single one of the thousands of spectators in the stadium.

I take a moment to look into the stands to experience the absolute joy, and when I turn back to the pitch, one of the players is leaping over the side boarding into my arms. It's one of the greatest moments I have experienced in my work with the many successful sports teams I have been lucky to be involved with.

We eventually get back to the dressing room. The passion and excitement are unbridled. This is something that we had worked towards for such a long time, and now it is here. These are magnificent moments. They are rare and special in any lifetime. As we take it all in, the cup in front of us, everyone begins to make their way to the team bus.

I am torn between two minds. A large part of me wants to go with this team to the bus and back to their town for what will be a magnificent homecoming, an incredible celebration of the entire community. There is also part of me that knows that, as myself and Miriam have just had our second baby, there is somewhere else I need to be.

Anybody who has had kids who seem to resist sleep knows the fun of trying to put some type of order on bedtime, especially when a new baby arrives in the house. Our little boy's sleep has been completely disrupted and, for the last few weeks, there has been very little sleep had by anyone, especially my wife, who's breastfeeding. Our son is trying to adjust to the new life in the house, the new energy and the new family dynamic, so he has been out of sorts and his routines have been equally out of kilter. His sleep is especially challenging at this moment.

This is why I was torn. Part of me wanted to kick back for the evening and just enjoy the sport, enjoy being with my friends; the other part knew that I was needed at home. I decided I would go home and put my little boy to bed. But if I am honest, a little part of me was frustrated, a part of me was resisting it.

One of my mates asked, 'Why don't you stay?' I gave a simple answer: 'I have to go home and put my boy to bed.' He knew there was a bit of hesitation, a bit of resistance. I was saying that I had to go home, and there was a part of me that was a little annoyed about that. My friend, being the great friend that he is and having four children himself, totally understood, but he also knew I was beginning to cause my own suffering. So after I said, 'I have to go home and put my boy to bed', he said, 'Why don't you reframe that?' 'Reframe what?' I asked. 'What you just said,' he replied.

A little annoyed, I said, 'But I have to go home. I have to put my little boy to bed.' I thought he was asking me to reframe it in a way that would permit me to stay and attend the home-coming celebrations. 'I can't stay,' I said.

171

'That's not what I'm saying,' replied my friend. **'Tell me that sentence again. Change nothing except the words "I have to" to "I get to".'**

I thought about it for a second. Slowly, I started to cop on. So I repeated the statement and this time I said, 'I get to go home and put my little boy to bed.'

He looked at me and said, 'One more time.'

Now the penny really dropped. I looked him in the eye and I said again, 'I get to go home and put my little boy to bed.'

Without even saying it, he was pulling me up and making sure I was taking my own medicine. He was telling me, 'Gerry, right now you are entering victim mode. Right now, you are causing your own suffering. You always have a choice. The options are to be here or to go home, and even if you don't really have a choice there, the choice you do have is how you feel about what you are doing.' He was reminding me that at times we can do things half-heartedly, we can do things that we have a choice to do or not to do, but the greatest choice we actually have is the stories we tell ourselves and the emotions we generate about the things we are doing.

Sometimes we need to change the entire story. Sometimes we simply need to change one word.

My reframing 'I have to put my little boy to bed' as 'I get to put my little boy to bed' changed everything. It made me remember how special, how precious and how amazing my little boy is and how lucky I am that I get to put him to bed.

Sometimes we all lose sight of things. I have lost sight of what really matters more times than I care to remember. But when I do, simply changing a word can be so important. It is something that has stuck with me for a long time. It is always on my mind as I tell myself a story about a situation.

Think about the stories you're telling yourself – about children, about work, about life. Sometimes we say we *have* to go to work, we *have* to go to a meeting, we *have* to go to the shops. When we say it in this way, our brain goes into a negative victim state. To say 'I have to' implies there's some form of resistance or that if you had a choice you would not choose to do it. **Regardless of whether you have a choice or not, reframing your story brings a sense of autonomy and empowerment.**

You can say things like:

* I get to go to work.

* I get to provide for my family.

* I get to go to the shop and buy food/clothes.

* I missed the bus and now I get to cycle or walk.

* I get to go see my parents.

* I get to put my kids to bed.

* I get to sing songs in the middle of the night with my kids.

When we change the way we speak about things, the things we speak about change. It's an amazing way of looking at life.

Stop 'butting' all over yourself

Changing 'I have to' to 'I get to' is so simple yet so powerful. It's a whole new way of taking yourself out of victim mode and putting yourself back into empowerment. It breeds a sense of autonomy, and human beings are set free only when we have a sense of purpose and mastery. If you give yourself back a renewed sense of autonomy, you give yourself back a renewed sense of empowerment and gratitude.

Neuroscience has brought us so many exceptional insights into the human brain over the last few decades, and one of the exciting findings is the concept of neuroplasticity. Neuroplasticity is the brain's ability to change its structure based on what we think about and what we speak about.

Neuroplasticity has proven beyond all doubt that the words we use and the things we think about constantly shape the structure of our brain and create new neurological circuits. These circuits are neurons that get wired together. The more different neurons become wired together, the more we are building thinking habits.

What neuroscience has also shown us is that in order for these circuits to be built, in order for the brain to actually respond, merely saying the words is not always enough. Neuroscience has shown us that the brain has an incredible intelligence to know when we really mean something, when we say something with real intent, and when we don't.

If we are sitting down and we say, 'Stand up', but we have no intention of standing up, we're just saying the words. Somehow our incredible brain knows that there is no intention behind that statement, and because it recognises this, it doesn't act, it doesn't fire. The brain can hear or say something, but the body, the nervous system, does not respond.

This awareness of how important it is to say things with real intent becomes particularly important when we think about not just the words we use, but also the intent behind them.

Our clever, intelligent brain, which is always scanning everything we say, needs to and wants to identify only the things we are thinking that have real intent behind them. And it will only act on those things. When we use the word 'but', the brain inherently knows that this word often means no action.

If we say, 'I want to go to the gym tomorrow, but I'm not sure if it will be open' or 'I want to get fit, but I don't like exercise' or 'I would love to be more calm, but meditation isn't for me', as soon as it hears the word 'but', the brain disregards the entire statement. It signifies to the brain that there is no real intent behind it. So, it doesn't build the new thinking habits that we require to execute that new behaviour. It doesn't fire the nervous system.

And without those neurons, without the nervous system being fired, we keep sleepwalking through life. We don't have the inner ambition to change, so as soon as we are met with even the slightest resistance or obstacle, we fall back into our old ways.

One of the simplest and quickest ways to short-circuit the brain is to use this principle of neuroscience. **To get the brain to act on a statement, we can use the word 'and' instead of 'but'.** The word 'and' has a completely different impact on the brain. The brain hears intent and activates new pathways that ignite our nervous system. It is now committing to movement – it is committing to action.

The next time you say, 'I would like to go to the gym', follow it with an 'and' statement: 'and I would like to get healthy'.

It is time that we acknowledge how our brain responds both physically and chemically to every word we use. From now on, replace all 'buts' with 'ands'. It's time we stop 'butting' all over our hopes, our dreams and our ambitions.

Stop the 'should', stop the guilt

When we use the word 'should', it means that we're looking back or reflecting on something, and we are judging what we did as somehow wrong – that maybe it was our fault for not taking another option.

If we say the word 'should' with an intention of learning, an intention of changing our behaviour, in that situation it isn't necessarily negative. If somebody says, 'I should have done something differently,' and they say that with the intention of actually doing something differently in the future, then that might be an empowering statement.

However, when most of us use the word 'should', there is some type of guilt attached to the statement. It's almost like a feeling of regret, where we believe we have let ourselves or others down or made a mistake that might have been avoided.

The more we use the word 'should', the more we imply that we had a choice that wasn't made, a course of action that wasn't pursued, and we 'should have known better'.

Listen to when and how many times you use the word 'should', and pay attention to the emotional reaction it evokes. So many times 'I should have' generates an emotion of anger or guilt. The word 'should' is often used about the past, but what we know about the past for certain is that it's uncontrollable. It's over. Yet the word 'should' makes us reflect on the past with judgement and a sense of guilt.

It is really important that when we look at the past, we use words such as 'I did'.

When we use affirming words, we own our actions, and we realise that maybe we simply did what we did based on the information or resources that were available at the time. And even though the decision we made might have turned out to be the wrong one, it was the decision we made based on what we knew then.

A word that can be of equally low quality is 'could'. When we use the words 'could have' or 'would have', the brain doesn't really hear an intent. 'Could have' and 'would have' are not the language of commitment or intention, so the brain gets confused and doesn't know whether this is a statement about something that is going to happen or not, a decision we are going to execute or not, something we are passionate about or not. So it doesn't really engage in any activity. It doesn't mobilise any action.

Over the years of working with and listening to some of the world's greatest performers, listening to their language, communication styles, habits, mechanisms and patterns, I have realised that the most high-performing people focus only on what they can control, and they let go of past mistakes easily and quickly. They also use affirming statements such as 'I am', 'I can', 'I will', 'I did', 'I have'. They don't use the words 'I could have', 'I should have', 'I would have'.

We need to make sure that we're using affirming words, words of high quality that nourish our nervous system and our soul. It's important we are using words that are based on intent. It's time to end the should, the could, the would, and replace them with the I am, I can, I will.

The power of the right question

Questions are an incredible method of communication. Anybody who is in the psychology or coaching business understands that sometimes the greatest way to help our clients is not to give them the answer, but to give them a better question. I believe that every single human being is one question away from a major breakthrough. The problem is that we're often asking ourselves the wrong question.

When we're faced with a difficult or challenging situation, we might ask ourselves questions like 'Can this work?' or 'What would happen if I fail?'

When we think about a challenge, no matter how difficult, an incredible question to ask is 'If I absolutely had to make this work, what would that look like?' Another way of asking this question is 'If this was possible, what would it require to get it done?'

Again, we're using the basic principle of neuroscience to use words to fire our intention, to fire the brain in a way that is no longer looking at our question as a threat, but as an opportunity.

Incredible questions lead to incredible awareness, and incredible awareness leads to incredible decisions and actions.

Whatever question you're asking yourself right now, write it down. Examine the words and the intention within it. Is the question giving awareness and attention to the problem or to the solution? Are the nature and the tone of the question implying that somehow there might be no solution? Is the question in some ways admitting defeat from the beginning? Or is it an empowering question, whereby the tone, nature and wording are committed to making it happen and making it work?

Every single person, team and organisation is one question away from a major breakthrough. Make sure you're asking yourself that question and make sure it's an empowering one. **Be aware that every word sparks an emotional response.**

So many times I hear people talking about massive challenges or massive meetings. Even the word 'massive' implies stress or pressure. Maybe instead of saying the challenge is 'massive', say it's 'incredible'. Now instead of 'I have a massive challenge', the sentence becomes 'I have an incredible challenge'. Instead of saying 'I have a massive meeting', say, 'I have a really exciting opportunity in this meeting.'

If we ignite our 'I can' statement with emotive intention, where we don't just say it in our heads, where it remains simply an intellectual thought, but where we say it with our hearts, if we replace 'but' with 'and', if we can be brave for 20 seconds, if we can refuse to allow the ego and the self-critic have the final say, if we don't let fear stand in our way and instead we make consistency our golden rule, where we look for the wins every day, where we reset every single morning and go again, where we continue to listen to our deepest wisdom and where we love ourselves enough to give ourselves a real shot at this one short incredible life, then that connection between intent and consistency gives us the incredible gift of opportunity and transformation.

CHAPTER 11
BUILDING HABITS

Consistency is the key to meaningful change

I hope by now that you have recognised you are capable of incredible change and that the steps to this incredible change are actually not that complicated. In fact, I absolutely believe that the path to even the most extraordinary achievement and change is paved with very ordinary steps that are within the grasp of most, if not all, people. Yet I am aware that, despite the steps to achievement and change being ordinary and achievable, most people don't actually make the change – or else they make it and then fall back into old habits. **Why is this? For me it comes down to one thing, the thing that sets the ordinary and the extraordinary apart: consistency.** The ability to consistently do simple things excellently and to consistently avoid distraction and procrastination is the key. We must find a way to motivate, inspire and create a consistent eagerness and ability to do the work.

Whatever dreams or goals you have – be that changing your career, becoming more confident or writing a book – you need a simple but powerful plan and activation map to keep you focused, determined and driven. This chapter will help you create this map and take the first steps, and in order to do that, we must avoid the goal-setting trap.

Avoiding the goal-setting trap

When we begin to set goals, it is important that we don't fall into the goal-setting trap. Far too many people have had the experience of setting important goals and abandoning them. At the moment you set them, you probably felt focused and motivated and confident that these goals would be actualised. However, as most of us have experienced, the vast majority of the goals we set never actually materialise. In fact, we get to a point where we even begin to resent the idea of goal setting.

While goal setting is meant to be motivating, inspiring and uplifting, sometimes the process of it brings emotions of guilt, shame and frustration because, for the vast majority of people, the goals they set are not actually achieved, and this leads us to feel even worse about ourselves.

So, we must remember that the golden rule in goal setting is that it's not actually about the goal. The real value of a goal is not simply in achieving the goal: the value and magic of a goal is the person it enables you to become.

When we set a goal, it is important that we break it into three sections:

1. The outcome
2. Process enablers
3. Become the person

We will use this table to work out how to achieve your goals. What you should include in each column is detailed below.

It's important we start by putting the goal at the end of the process, as below. Once we write down the goal, we then work back to the second step, which is the process enablers, and then back to the first step, which is to identify the type of person that would be able to achieve your goals. Here's an example:

Characteristics of a person who would achieve these goals	Process enablers	Goals
1. Organised 2. Disciplined 3. Assertive	1. Bring my own lunch to work 2. Keep a spending journal to identify spending habits 3. Cancel all subscriptions I'm not making use of	I want to have more money
1. Organised 2. Productive with their time 3. Confident to say no to people and things that waste their time 4. Strong emotional boundaries	1. Plan my week, starting by inserting 30 minutes every day that I'm going to take for myself 2. Cut out or cut down social media for a month (possibly uninstall it from my phone) 3. Say no quickly to the things I don't want to be involved in	I want to have more time to do things I love

1. The outcome

What is the outcome you would like to achieve? Perhaps this outcome is to have more money, to fall in love or to become fitter and healthier. It could be anything, but the approach is the same.

Once you have those outcomes written, we can begin the second and more important part of the goal setting.

2. Identify the process enablers

Beside each of the goals, whether that is, for example, to manifest more money or to fall in love or to become fit and healthy, write down the process enablers. Aim for three. A process enabler is a simple action that you could take every day that will move you closer to your goal.

So, if your goal is to become fit and healthy, you could write down one thing that's going to move your body, one thing you could do to improve your diet, and one thing you can improve about your sleep.

When we turn the focus away from the outcome and onto the process, it gives us real, tangible, measurable activities that we can do every day. The more we complete these simple tasks, the further we move towards our desired goals.

By having practical process enablers, we begin to build feelings of motivation, success and confidence.

3. Become the person

The third and, by far, the most important part of goal setting is to think about the type of person who has already achieved the things you want.

I AM. I CAN. I WILL.

Now it's your turn:

Characteristics of a person who would achieve these goals	Process enablers	Goals

Visualisation

An audio recording in which I guide you through a visualis-ation for this step can be accessed on my website https://www.gerryhussey.ie/i-am-i-can-i-will-meditations with the password IAMICANIWILL.

In this visualisation, we will focus on identifying the type of person that we can become that is most likely to lead us to achieve our deepest dreams and ambitions.

Far too often, people focus on the outcome, or they focus on the process, but the success of the process and the outcome is also dependent on us being the right person with the right mindset and the right emotions as we pursue the process.

Even if we have the right process and we know the outcome we desire, if we are pursuing both process and outcome in the wrong emotional state or with the wrong mindset, we are now putting a block in our own path. My deepest learning and understanding about how manifesta-tion really works is that yes, we need a clear outcome, and yes, we need a clear process, but more importantly, we need to be turning up each and every day as the right person with the right mindset, sending out the right message and frequency to the universe and living each day in the right emotional state as if we have already achieved our dreams.

This visualisation will help you each morning to get into that correct mindset and emotional space where you can think, act and feel in a powerful way that will allow you to manifest your dreams with greater ease.

So, let's begin; firstly, I'll ask you to close your eyes. With our eyes closed, we are going to manifest an inner image of the things we want to achieve, see them with great clarity, and focus on the details.

As you continue to bring these desired outcomes into your mind, we now slowly begin to imagine the type of person that would have all of these things in their life. Imagine the person who has already achieved all the things you dream of standing in front of you. Observe them, notice them, observe their body language. It's probably strong, calm and assured.

For a moment now, just focus on their body language, making a mental image of the big and little details of how they stand and how they physically interact and communicate with the world and with others. Notice all the big and little things about their body language. Notice how they stand, their relaxed but strong shoulders, their calm but intent gaze, their gentle but focused facial expressions.

Our body language communicates so much about our intent and about the type of person we are, so it is important that we begin to consciously align our daily body language with the type of person who lives with confidence, clarity, focus and joy.

Now that you have a mental image of this, it will become the blueprint of the new body language that you will display on a daily basis.

Now, as you observe this person, I want you to notice how they speak. I want you to notice the tone of their voice: it's calm but assured. I want you to notice the words they use; they are powerful, uplifting and assertive.

Focus on the things that they are speaking about. Notice they speak only about the things they can control. Notice they speak only about solutions, and they speak only about people that are in their company.

Really become aware that there is something powerful about the way they communicate. It is strong but calm, it is focused and assertive. Now visualise yourself speaking with the same calmness, with the same intention and with the same focus.

To manifest the things that you dream of, you must be willing to become a powerful communicator who speaks only about the things they want to experience, the things they love, not the things they fear, who uses empowering words and sentences and speaks about incredible abilities, not other people. Let's visualise ourselves becoming powerful communicators.

Now, I would like you to visualise this person sitting at home. They are at ease in a beautiful, love-filled home. I want you to experience the sense of gratefulness and joy that they experience while they take time to acknowledge the wonderful things they have in their life.

Now, I want you to take these feelings and make them your own; I want you to feel right now as if you have already achieved these outcomes. I want you to embody the emotions as if your dreams have already happened.

As you hold these images, I would like you to focus on your powerful breath. With each inhale, we breathe in your new power and your new focus. And with each exhale, we release fear. We release limiting beliefs.

It's time to become the person; it is time to become a person of focus, clarity, gratitude, joy and empowerment.

Visualise yourself walking and speaking, feeling empowered and unstoppable. It is important to remember that where our attention goes, energy flows, and the things that we give our energy to are the things that become more abundant in our life.

So, let's give our energy, awareness and attention to becoming a person who is capable and powerful and confident and grateful. Let's give our energy, awareness and attention to becoming the person who has already achieved the goals you dream of: the right person with the right process achieves the right outcome. Today we step into becoming the right person.

*

Now close your eyes for a moment and think about somebody who has an abundance of money, who is fit and healthy or who is deeply in love – whatever your goal might be. Can you visualise that person?

What would they look like?

Now think about the characteristics that person would have. For example, do you think that person would be organised, would they be confident, would they be disciplined, would they be assured? What type of people would they surround themselves with? Would they be positive? Would they be fun to be around?

Let's write them down.

_____

_____

_____

_____

If you were to describe yourself right now, would you use any of these characteristics? If not, this is where we get stuck: this is where goal setting fails. As I said before, life does not give us what we want; life gives us who we are.

Setting a goal but staying the same person simply does not work. That's why step three is so important. Your ability to actualise your goal has very little to do with the goal itself, but more to do with the person y ou choose to become.

Your first and most important step in goal setting is not to focus on the outcome, but to become the right person with the right process. Once you become the person who thinks and feels and acts in the right way, then you have the right process. The right person with the right process never worries about the outcome.

Perhaps you do already have some of the characteristics you listed, but there might be gaps. The main thing is to not punish yourself about it or say, 'This means I can never achieve my goals' – remember what we spoke about in the last section: you CAN. Now it's time for 'I WILL'. You can see these 'gaps' as an action list, and you can break them down into micro goals so you can achieve your dream. If you need to be more organised, how might you do that? If finding the time to exercise or write or study has held you back from your goals in the past, what simple, practical steps can you take to carve out that time for yourself?

Goal setting is not about the goal: it is about liberating yourself. It's about overcoming your self-doubt and facing your fears. It's about backing yourself and having fun along the way. Goals should be things that awaken us, inspire us and change us for the better. If they do, we quickly realise that the magic is actually in the process, the liberation is in daring, and the happiness lies in the ability to go after your deepest dreams without making those dreams your master.

CHAPTER 12
KEEP EDITING,
KEEP ENHANCING

Creating statements to live by

It is now time to turn the work back to you again. In this chapter, we are going to prepare affirming statements that will give us the courage, confidence and consistency to uphold our empowered sense of self as we move through the many challenges that life involves.

These 'I will' statements are promises that we are making to ourselves. They are new and powerful commitments that take our energy, awareness and attention away from everything and everybody we can't control and place it back on what we can control, which is our response.

These 'I will' statements give us back our sense of autonomy and control. These 'I will' statements are about allowing ourselves to step into our power and our light.

There is nothing enlightened about shrinking ourselves so that others won't feel insecure around us, and these 'I will' statements will challenge you to step into your power with more clarity and certainty and not retreat when you meet challenges.

It is time

It is time to stop shrinking, it is time to stop apologising for your dreams and your abilities, it is time to stop second-guessing yourself, and it is time to stop playing small so that others won't feel insecure around you.

Life, your life, was never about other people; it was never about other people's expectations of you; it was never about what other people believe about you. Your life has only ever been and will only ever be about you, about who you say you are, about the freedom you are willing to give yourself and the light and truth that you are willing to step into.

The moment we become enough for ourselves, the moment we look in the mirror and see someone who inspires us and uplifts us, the moment we are enough for ourselves is the moment we become free.

These 'I will' statements are the promises we are making to ourselves, to our inner child, to that eight-year-old self. We are saying, 'I will protect you, I will stand up for you, I will honour you, and I will set you free.' It is time that 'I should' becomes 'I will'; it is time that 'I could' becomes 'I will.'

It is time to set yourself free.

When I hear my inner critic being hard on myself, I WILL:

1. _____

2. _____

3. _____

I AM. I CAN. I WILL.

When I hear myself playing myself or my dreams down, I WILL:

1. _____
2. _____
3. _____

When I catch myself telling myself an unhelpful inner story, I WILL:

1. _____
2. _____
3. _____

When at times I get things wrong, I WILL:

1. _____
2. _____
3. _____

When I feel my emotional boundaries are being dismissed or ignored, I WILL:

1. _____
2. _____
3. _____

In order to have real and meaningful relationships, I WILL:

1. _____
2. _____
3. _____

If I am in a relationship where I am not allowed to be my true self, I WILL:

1. _____
2. _____
3. _____

If someone doesn't treat me with respect, I WILL:

1. _____
2. _____
3. _____

When I am faced with an important challenge, I WILL:

1. _____
2. _____
3. _____

If I encounter setbacks, I WILL:

1. _____
2. _____
3. _____

From now on, when I speak my truth, I WILL:

1. _____
2. _____
3. _____

TIME TO DO SOME WORK

Practical exercise: vision board

Now let's turn the work over to you for the final time. In this exercise, we're going to focus on the life, the characteristics and the things that we will manifest.

Sometimes, the greatest obstacle to achieving our goals is a lack of vision. Most people can be uncertain about exactly what they want, and they might struggle to express it with absolute certainty. Others might have a level of certainty, but in the adversity of their everyday lives they can get distracted and pulled away from their dreams.

The greater the vision, the clearer and more specific it is, and the more regularly we revisit it, the more likely we are to manifest it.

When we have a clear understanding of the different elements that we want to achieve and experience in our personal and professional lives, we can use techniques such as visualisation, meditation, journaling and affirmations to consistently focus our conscious and unconscious attention and awareness on seeking out and finding the people, situations and opportunities that bring us closer to this reality.

A good way of doing this is by creating a vision board. A vision board, when properly used, is a powerful 'I will' statement. It is a clear set of images and words that identify the future life we want to create, the future characteristics we want to possess and the future situations we want to experience.

Earlier in this book, we spoke about the power of our subconscious programs and how when we speak and think about a certain reality over and over again, it becomes encoded into these subconscious programs. When we do this, we convince ourselves that this is a new reality waiting to happen. Then the reticular activating system of the brain seeks out and identifies cues and realities that connect with our subconscious programs. By having a clear vision board, we can begin to see and experience our future as if it has already happened.

Our vision board becomes our strategic filter

I have used vision boards all my life. I use them for both my personal life and my professional life, and I always have a clear picture, which becomes my strategic filter. At various times along the path, new or different opportunities will come into my life, and I use this vision board to help me decide which opportunities I take and which ones I don't. I ask myself if this new opportunity brings me closer to this picture or not. I say yes to everything that moves me closer to making that picture a reality and no to everything that moves me away from it.

A vision board gives context and meaning to every decision. Very often my decision to say no to things makes no sense to other people because they can't see the end goal.

A vision board for me is a powerful affirmation. It is a tool to prime our subconscious programs.

Once the vision board is created, each morning look at it and repeat affirming 'I will' statements that relate to every image on the board. So, if you have a picture of a house by the sea, every morning you will repeat to yourself, 'I will live in a beautiful house by the sea'. If your vision board has a picture of a wedding ring, then you might say, 'I will fall deeply in love with the most amazing partner'. If the vision board has a picture of somewhere spectacular that you want to visit, the affirmation could be 'I will give myself permission to follow my dreams and explore this incredible universe'.

The vision board not only becomes a focus point, it also becomes an inner compass – the direction your life will move in. The more certain we become about the direction our life will move in, the less energy and attention we give to where we don't want it to go. This vision board becomes your daily navigation tool.

When we experience the 'why' in our hearts, the 'how' appears in our world

The key to maximising the power of a vision board is to feel the emotions of excitement and joy as if you have already experienced the situation. Repeat your 'I will' statements without the need to plan or allowing self-doubt to creep in. It is important that first, we have the vision, and second, we experience the feelings of joy, love and gratitude.

Once we know why we want these visions, once we stay connected to that powerful, emotive 'why' that brings our soul alive, the 'how' will follow. Some people make the mistake of getting lost trying to think about how they can make this work, and because they don't immediately have a plan or they can't imagine a situation that would allow these dreams to manifest, they think that their dream is too big or outside of their capability. I have no idea how I will manifest the dreams I put on my vision board or when they will come to pass. But I trust that I will somehow find a way to manifest these goals. The vision board is a way of igniting the part of you that says 'I will'. And once we are in this powerful state of 'I will', once we know why these goals are so important, then we will find the 'how'.

Try not to become consumed with having a perfect plan or timeline. As co-creators in this universe, we sometimes have to work *with* the universe. I've had to be patient at times. I've had to dare to take the first step, even when I couldn't see the second step, but I never doubted for a moment that these things would happen. A vision board is a statement that says, 'I will back myself, I will back my dreams'. Trust that the universe will align, and when it does, take those opportunities. Do not wait until you have the perfect plan. Dream daily and dream big. Dream with your soul, dream with your heart, and allow everything else to unfold as it needs to unfold.

Refresh it regularly

The final step is to regularly update your vision board. As we achieve various goals and our life transitions, stop and replace an image; a new picture, a new word, keeps the vision board fresh. Keep editing your vision board to keep it alive, exciting and relevant to the dreams and hopes that you have right now.

Vision boards are not something that we wish for. They are something we look at with absolute intent, knowing that we will manifest those things. We have a renewed determination every single morning that our life will go in the direction of our dreams, that we will have the power to overcome any obstacle that might come along the way, that we will have the resilience to deal with setbacks. It is a way of giving ourselves the freedom to step firmly with courage in the direction of our dreams. It says, 'This is the life I will create. These are the images I will experience. These are the words and characteristics that will define me.'

Now open your heart and mind, put fear aside, and create a vision board that inspires and sets your dreams free. This is your one short, beautiful life – it is not a dress rehearsal. Stop waiting, stop playing small and start living your dreams by saying, 'I WILL'.

Meditation

A new daily mantra

An audio recording in which I guide you through this meditation can be accessed on my website https://wwwgerry hussey.ie/i-am-i-can-i-will-meditations with the password IAMICANIWILL.

Begin to notice your breathing. Notice that rich, life-giving oxygen as it enters the body, renewing your cells, your genes, renewing the life-force within you, and as you exhale, allow the old energy to be moved away from the body.

Breathing is a beautiful technique involving three key parts: the inhale, where we take in the new; the exhale, where we release the old; and the pause between the inhale and exhale, and again between the exhale and the new inhale.

Too often we focus on the inhale and the exhale. So now let's focus on all three dimensions: that life-giving inhale, then pause, that beautiful space between the no longer and the not yet, that pause that gives us depth and meaning.

And now let's release. That beautiful letting go. Breathing is the same as life. Each morning we wake up, we take on new ideas, new thinking, new challenges. Regularly throughout the day, we stop to reset, to get perspective, to observe our awareness and attention, and at the end of every day, we release. Let's continue this for just a few moments. Follow that beautiful breath as it enters, pauses and then releases.

As we follow this breath, begin to let your shoulders and neck relax and release any tension that you've been carrying. Leave it down for now. Maybe your body is tense because it is physically tired, or maybe the tension, the weight you are experiencing in your body, is an emotional weight. Are you carrying the weight of the world on your shoulders? Are you carrying the weight of other people's expectations? Are you still carrying the weight of the past?

Now it is time to let that go, so as we breathe, as we release the tension from our neck and shoulders, we are symbolically releasing the weight of expectations, the weight of the past. We are letting go of the weight of the need to understand, predict or control the future; we are letting it go so that we can simply be.

And now, as we begin to enter this present moment, let's repeat some 'I will' affirmations.

I will allow myself more time and space for me.
I will prioritise my hopes, my dreams and my health.
I will stand up for what I believe in.

I will be fearless in the pursuit of my dreams.

I will be unapologetic for being my true self.

I will speak to myself with kindness and love.

I will not allow my self-critic to have the final word. I will allow my inner coach to speak with courage and confidence.

I will treat others with kindness and love.

I will not allow judgement, comparison or criticism to be part of who I am.

I will no longer focus on my environment or the things I cannot control. I will focus only on the freedom I have to choose my response.

I will be me. I will be powerful. I will be free.

Now, let's continue to breathe for just a few more moments, allowing that new empowered speech to come alive inside, allowing that inner coach to wake up, allowing the apologies to disappear, and allowing passion to appear.

You are more powerful than you think. You are more loved than you can ever imagine, and you are free to be whoever you choose to be. It is time to focus on what we have and what we want. It is time to say, 'I will'.

Slowly, we finish our short meditation with one final deep breath. And as we breathe in that new energy, that new life, that new you, we welcome all exactly as it is, and we allow ourselves to be at peace with what is, to be at one with what is.

And from this place of peace and ease, we say, 'I will'.

Summary of Section 3: I Will

*   Give yourself a different perspective on the situation.

*   Goal setting is less about the goal and more about the person you will become.

*   Intent is the key to real change.

*   You are one question away from a major breakthrough, as long as you're asking yourself the right question.

IT'S OVER TO YOU

I hope this book will be a constant guide that you can return to again and again to see if you're living from a place of power, love and joy, or if maybe your stories have slipped back into fear. Sit down on a regular basis with this book to renew and edit your stories, your dreams, your goals. Life is always changing. We are never the same person two days in a row.

There is a beautiful expression that says, 'No man ever steps in the same river twice, for it's not the same river, and he's not the same man.' This tells us that all of life is renewing and changing, so the more regularly we sit down to reassess where we are, what we think about and where we're giving our energy to, the more we live a life of vitality – the more we have a win mindset.

What's important now? PMA stands for 'present moment awareness', which is the technique of bringing ourselves into the present, where we take our energy, awareness and attention away from everything we can't control and place it firmly on what we can control – our thoughts and our emotions. PMA allows us to take our energy, awareness and attention away from our point of pain and the things that deplete our confidence, our passion and our energy, and instead place them back on a point of power, on the things that give us a sense of courage, empowerment and freedom.

You are a magnificent, ever-evolving process of change, so allow yourself to embrace change with ease and excitement. Don't resist it or fight it. Instead, put your energy into creating the change you want and becoming the person that makes you proud.

ACKNOWLEDGEMENTS

To my mum, your love, care and hugs are among the greatest gifts in this universe. You have given me wings to fly and roots to be strong. Of all the treasures in the world, a mug of tea with you has always been and will always be the greatest medicine. I love you with all my heart.

To my dad, my pillar of courage and strength, you are my hero. Every minute we spend travelling together, every talk and every session we get to do together – you may never know how important your presence has been for every step of my journey. We are only getting started. I love you more than I can ever say.

To my family, for every moment of care, support and love, for being in my corner even when I may have forgotten it. Thank you from the bottom of my heart.

To Teresa Daly and all the team at Gill. Thank you for believing in me. Thank you for the passion you radiate and thank you for helping me believe I could write a book like this, a short, beautiful, impactful book where the lessons come fast and where the readers feel awakened and empowered.

ACKNOWLEDGEMENTS

I wanted it to be 'punchy' and you allowed and encouraged me to go after it.

Catherine Gough, there are very few people I have ever enjoyed working with as much as you. You made it fun and enjoyable, and your support and guidance are truly a gift for all lucky enough to have you in their corner.

To all the incredible clients that I have had the extreme pleasure and fortune to know and work with, thank you for trusting me, thank you for challenging me, thank you for allowing me grow.

Ravi, thank you for your constant love, wisdom and understanding. You have taught me more than I even know.

To Miriam, you are my sun, my moon and my North Star. Without you I am lost at sea. With you I always know the way home. Thank you for illuminating my world and our home. You are our true North Star.

To Elijah and Bethany, the two greatest gifts and the greatest love I could ever dare to know. Dream with all your hearts and believe with all your souls.

NOTES:

NOTES:

NOTES:

NOTES:

NOTES:

NOTES:

NOTES:

NOTES:

NOTES:

NOTES: